## CharismaLife
### PUBLISHERS ®
### Lake Mary, Florida

Stephen Strang
*President*

David W. Welday III
*Publisher*

Jerry Lenz
*Editor*

Cindy Carter
*Editorial Assistant*

Jeanne Merola
*Prepress Manager*

Cathleen Kwas
*Prepress Coordinator*

Jennifer Bouw
*Production Coordinator*

Sandy Wright
*Copy Editor*

Cynthia Terrio
*Royalties and Copyrights*

Bill Johnson, Mark McIntyre, Diane Vivian
*Contributing Artists*

Library of Congress Catalog Card Number: 94-74022

International Standard Book Number: 1-57405-001-X

# POWER PAK OF OBJECT LESSONS

## Compiled by the Editors of KIDS Church

It's a fact that we remember more when we **see and hear** something. That's why object lessons are such a great tool to help young kids understand abstract spiritual truths. By weaving a lesson around a simple object, you enable kids to make a connection between the two. As in a parable, a common object is best. Jesus used many parables to teach. Let Him be our model.

***Power Pak of Object Lessons*** offers 100 creative ideas in an easy-to-follow lesson format. Here are a few tips for getting the most out of these illustrations:

- Plan ahead.
- Review the objects needed a week or two in advance.
- Don't rush around at the last minute to find the objects.
- Search the categories carefully to pick just the right message.
- And remember...the purpose of the object is to drive the point home. Keep your focus on the truth you are trying to convey.

# TABLE OF CONTENTS

## Evangelism

## Faith/Salvation

## Giving

## God's Word

## Prayer

## Sin

## Warfare

*Object Lessons can be a powerful and exciting addition to your children's church program. We have developed a full-line of wonderful children's church programs called KIDS Church (Kids In Divine Service).*

*If you'd like more information about these resources, contact your local Christian bookstore or call us at 1-800-451-4598.*

## PROCEDURE

### Operation World

**The Point:** Tell the world about Jesus.

**Props:** Globe. (The larger the better. There is a 4-foot inflatable globe available at many discount stores for under $10.00, or order the Prayer Globall through CharismaLife. Call 1-800-451-4598.)

Every soldier has an objective, a mission, a job to do. As soldiers in God's Army, we have a mission to share His love with the world. When Jesus was on this earth, He healed and delivered people and then was killed, but He rose again from death to save man. Before Jesus went to His Father in heaven, our Commander in Chief (JESUS) gave those of us in His Army our orders. He told us that we must tell the world what He has done for us. Our job as soldiers in God's Army is to tell as many people as we can about what our Commander in Chief, Jesus, has done for us and that they can be part of God's Army, too.

This globe represents the world. While you may not be able to literally travel to the other countries of the world, you can have an impact by praying for people in other parts of our world. As I toss this globe out to you, look and see what country is right under your hand when you catch it. Stand up and pray that the Holy Spirit would lead those people to Jesus. *(Toss the globe out to a child, have him pray for the people of a nation and toss the globe back to you. Repeat as you feel is appropriate.)*

## PREPARATION

**M**ake a huge map of the world (accuracy is not important) with a red dot in the center.

## PROCEDURE

### Our Mission: The World

**The Point:** Because of Calvary, God's army is victorious.

**Props:** World map (or roll of brown shipping paper) and colored markers.

Napoleon, a famous general and commander, once brought his best men around a table as he laid out a map of the world. He was emotional, both angry and sad. He pointed to the red dot in the center, which was a town called Waterloo. He said, "If it had not been for this very place that we failed to conquer, we could have taken the whole world." It was his place of doom. It is where his army lost the battle.

Probably the enemy, the devil, has gathered all of his demons around a map and said the same thing. (Roll out the map.) "If it had not been for this place called 'Calvary' where Jesus died, we could have deceived the whole world. But this place was our downfall."

Now God's army can gather in a class like this and spread out a world map. We can point to this spot in the very center. (Hold up the map.) Because of Calvary, because Jesus died and came back to life, we have the assurance of victory. We can go out and tell the whole world that our side wins in the end! Because of Jesus, God's army will never know defeat. Our last command, our last line of duty, is to go into all the world and win them to God's side and baptize them in the name of the Father, Son and Holy Spirit.

## PROCEDURE

**The Great Commission**

**The Point:** We all have a part in God's Great Commission.

**Props:** Scroll certificates for each boy or girl with maps (any kind of street map) pasted on them.

Today, God's army is receiving the Great Commission. Each Christian soldier is assigned to go to the world. You are to make disciples and enlist soldiers for God wherever you go.

You have been through training. You have the armor of God and the Holy Spirit inside of you. Now it is time to use what you have learned. *(Call each boy and girl forward, one at a time, by name. Present them their Great Commission Scroll. Please have several scrolls for visitors.)*

You can start by inviting someone in your neighborhood to church with you next week. We have Good News to give to the world. We are supposed to conquer the world, not taking prisoners, but giving them a greater life.

You are not alone. The Holy Spirit will help you get people to come to the Lord. When you enlist others, you are fulfilling your duty as a Christian soldier. This is the Great Commission given by Jesus.

This recruiting plan works. It has worked for almost 2,000 years. It is a worldwide plan. It will continue to be successful until Jesus comes back to earth to take all of God's army to our eternal base in the heavenly city. If we fulfill the Great Commission, there will be many, many who experience the joy and excitement of joining God's army.

*(Please note that in a large Kids Church you will need to plan this well in advance.)*

## PREPARATION

**M**ake a giant calendar for next month out of the posterboard. Leave enough space to write something for each day.

## PROCEDURE

## Plan Ahead

**The Point:** Plan with Jesus and pray.

**Props:** Marker and posterboard.

We use a calendar to plan ahead for things we want to do, but let's use this prayer calendar to plan to share God's love with people we know.

*(Write someone's name down on a date.)* Each night before you go to bed, write down the name of someone you want to share God's love with the next day. *(Write another name on a different date.)* There may be someone in your family you need to do something special for, or someone in your neighborhood you would like to talk to about the Lord. *(Write Mr. Johnson in a different date.)* Maybe someone you go to school with needs to know about Jesus. *(Write a boy or girl's name on a different date.)* Plan ahead! You can make good things happen in your future. Jesus gave us the command, "Go! Baptize them and teach them to obey!"

Think of some very good things you can do tomorrow that could cause someone to want to know the Lord. You can win friends by being a friend to them. We plan our future by filling in the calendar daily. Each day that you are successful in doing what you planned to do, give yourself a little star or a smiley face in the box for that day. *(Draw a happy face.)*

Don't forget to pray over your plans. Kneel by your bed with your calendar of events and ask the Lord to help you as you try to obey His command for the next day.

## Procedure

### Golf Talk

**The Point:** We can point people toward God.

**Props:** Golf ball, putter and can (or bucket) you can hit the ball into.

Our speech should guide others to Jesus. I have here a golf ball, and we are going to let it represent a person who needs to get into heaven. The can is going to represent heaven. This club is going to represent us. The object of golf is to hit the ball into the hole using a golf club. If you hit the ball wrong, it does not go into the hole. You keep trying until it gets there. *(Set up a 5-foot putt.)*

I am going to try to guide this ball into the hole. *(Try it. If you make it, cheer. If you miss, say "Oops! Guess I'll try again.")* As Christians, we should be trying to guide people into heaven, and one way we do that is by what we say. If our friends hear us talking about how important it is to love Jesus and invite Him into our hearts, they'll be hearing about how to get to heaven, and that's good! But if they hear us using bad words and see us doing wrong things, we're not guiding them toward heaven, and they may not get there. We teach others by our words. Let's check over what we are saying and make sure we are pointing people toward heaven. *(Have a few kids try hitting the ball into the can.)*

Evangelism

## Jesus' Love Bubbling Over

**The Point:** Let the love of Jesus overflow to others.

**Props:** Bottle of bubble solution.

## PROCEDURE

Jesus wants His love to be bubbling out of your life and into others. You may ask, "How can that happen?" Well, first you must have Jesus in you. You must have asked Jesus to come into your heart and forgive you of all your sins. *(Hold up bottle of bubble solution.)* This bottle represents a life which is full of Jesus—one whose sins are forgiven.

Now that we have Jesus in our hearts, God wants us to share that with others. If we just keep it to ourselves, we're not doing our part. If I did not blow bubbles with this, it would not be doing what it was made to do. You and I, once Jesus came into our lives, were made to share Him with others.

You still may ask, "How can I do that?" Well, you could tell a friend at school about Jesus. *(Blow one bubble.)* That would be a way. You could invite someone to come to church. *(Blow another bubble.)*

Did you know that as you give your offering you are letting God's love bubble out of you? Giving is a way to say, "I am going to let God's love bubble to others." *(Blow a bunch of bubbles.)*

This offering is taken and put with other offerings and together they can be used to share God's love with many. *(Blow more bubbles.)* So as you think about giving today, think about letting God's love bubble over to others.

*(If you know the song "Jesus' Love Is a Bubbling Over," sing it while you take the offering.)*

## PROCEDURE

**Light a Candle**

**The Point:** We must let our lights shine for Jesus.

**Props:** Set of six to ten large candles and six to ten volunteers, depending on the size of your group.

Give one of your helpers the candles and matches. Your helper will give children candles as they walk up front. Have them stand in line at the front of the room. When you begin talking, have your helper light one candle. Then turn off the lights. That child will then light the candle of the next person in line, who will light the next candle, until all the candles are lit.

Jesus says not to keep our light under a bushel. Instead, we are to be a light. *(Helper lights one candle. Lights are shut off.)* Now one light doesn't look like it's much, but as we pass it on, it becomes brighter and brighter. *(Kids are lighting one another's candles.)* This is how sharing the gospel is. As we share it with other people and they become Christians, the light becomes brighter. Society notices it, and things change. The darkness lessens as the light becomes brighter.

Each of you is a light. As you share the light of Jesus Christ within you with other people, you are making an impact on other people's lives. Let's be a light for each other and for our friends. *(Have one of the children close this lesson with a prayer that we would be lights.)*

## PREPARATION

**A**ttach the hearts to the candles with masking tape.

## PROCEDURE

### Hearts on Fire

**The Point:** Our kindness will draw others to Jesus.

**Props:** Two tall candles, two candle holders, two red posterboard hearts, masking tape and matches.

I want to tell you about the greatest act of kindness you can do.*(Display the hearts. Light one of the candles.)* Imagine this candle is you. Because you are a Christian, the Bible says you are the "light of the world." That means you have the light of God's love in your heart. Jesus is living in you, which means love is alive in you.

But there are many kids in our town who do not have the light of God's love living in them. *(Point to the other heart.)* They are still in the darkness of sin. What is the greatest act of kindness you can show them? Well, you can and should show them God's love in simple ways, like sharing cookies, but that's not the greatest act of kindness.

The greatest act of kindness you can do for such a person is tell her about Jesus. Tell her how Jesus died on the cross for her sins, rose again and wants to take her to heaven.

When you tell others about Jesus, God might use the light of your witness to bring them to forgiveness and salvation. (Use the flame of the first candle to light the second candle.) Because of your witness, others might accept Jesus and gain eternal life! Wow!

It isn't that you have the power to save anyone from their sins. Only God can do that. But He can use you and your kindness to help make it happen, and that's the kindest act of all.

## The Pardon

**The Point:** Jesus paid the price for our freedom.

**Props:** Picture (or photo) of prison and letter signed "Jesus" in envelope.

### PROCEDURE

**K**ids, how many of you have even been inside a prison? I'm sure some of you have watched TV shows or movies about people in prison. *(Hold up picture.)* The reason people go to prison is because they have done something so bad that they must be punished. When they are arrested, they are brought before a judge and given a sentence if they are convicted of a crime.

Once they are imprisoned, they can't go anywhere. Sometimes criminals are sentenced to death because they committed a really terrible crime. When they are on death row, the only thing that can save them from the death sentence is a pardon from the governor. The governor writes a letter that sets the prisoner free.

Kids, because of our sin we are under a death sentence. The Bible says that the penalty of sin is death. But there is one more powerful than any governor, who can grant us a pardon. Jesus has already served our prison time for us. He has removed the death sentence from our lives.

Jesus has paid the price for our freedom. When we accept Jesus as our Savior, we are granted a pardon. *(Show letter signed by Jesus.)* We are pardoned from serving an eternity in hell.

## PROCEDURE

### Will You Marry Me?

**The Point:** If we accept Jesus, we will live with Him forever.

**Props:** Engagement ring.

**W**hen you make a promise, you are giving a guarantee that you are going to do what you say. One promise sometimes made is between young men and women. Young men who want to marry their sweethearts give them a diamond ring, called an engagement ring. *(Show the ring.)*

The ring then becomes a symbol of their promise. It is a guarantee from the young man that he wants to spend the rest of his life with the lady. When she accepts the ring and wears it, she makes the same promise. She will marry no one else and will spend the rest of her life with the man.

This engagement ring says these two people promise to give themselves to each other and be together for the rest of their lives.

God also wants to be with us forever. He said so 2,000 years ago when He sent His only Son, Jesus, to us. It's a promise. If we accept God's promise, Jesus, then we can live with Him forever in eternity.

# Gospills

**PROCEDURE**

**The Point:** The gospel is the best medicine in the world.

**Props:** A medicine bottle labeled "Gospills."

Boys and girls, this is a miracle drug prescription. *(Hold up "Gospills" bottle.)* You would think it is very expensive. Some people spend almost everything they make on prescription medicine. You might also ask, "Is this a proven drug?" Our Federal Drug Administration does not allow doctors to prescribe drugs which haven't been tried and proven for safety.

You might ask, "How much do you take of this medicine? Should you take a dose after every meal, or one dose in the morning and another at bedtime?"

This medicine is not expensive. Even the very poor can afford it. It's not new. It has been proven effective for almost 2,000 years. It has never failed. It has been put to the test more than any other remedy known to man. God prescribes a dosage four times a day. He says in effect, "Parents, give it to your children when they wake up, when they sit down, when they walk by the way, and when they lie down" (Deut. 6:6-7).

And what about the taste? Oh, it is sweeter than honey. And you can't overdose. Too much medicine can kill a person, you know. But the more you take of this, the better you get! That's the Gospill truth! The Gospill actually represents the gospel. Gospel is Greek for good news, which is the Good News of Jesus Christ. The Good News of Jesus Christ is the best medicine.

## The Jail of Sin

**The Point:** Faith in Jesus sets us free.

**Props:** Large cardboard box.

## PREPARATION

Cut out a jail cell with a door and door lock. Cut out two large keys, but only one to fit the door lock. Label the jail cell "The Jail of Sin." Label the key that fits the door lock "Faith Key" and the other "Law Key"

## PROCEDURE

God had to issue laws and commands because people became so wicked. But the more rules He made, the worse they became. People just wouldn't live the way God planned for them to live. Finally God said, "The people of My creation have become prisoners in a jail of their own sin. The law cannot set them free from their wickedness." *(Try the Law key on the lock. Show that it will not work. It may be too big to fit in the lock.)*

Then Jesus came. He had a new law and a new key. It is called "The Law of the Spirit of Life in Christ Jesus." Because Abraham had faith and believed God's Word, God promised to send Jesus. Jesus came to deliver people from the curse that sin brings and set them free with the "Law of the Spirit of Life." *(Try the Faith key. It opens the door.)* Faith unlocks the door to sin's jail. God is looking for our faith in Jesus to release us from the jail of sin. Jesus offers us the key. Take it by faith.

## The Draft Letter

**The Point:** We're invited to join God's army.

**Props:** Envelope, stamp, paper and pen.

## PREPARATION

Copy the following letter and place it in the addressed, stamped envelope.

*Dear _____,*

*I want to invite you to become a part of the most powerful army ever put together in this world. My army is a winner! With Me as the Commander in Chief, we have never lost a battle.*

*The battle between good and evil is growing bigger and bigger every day, and I need some good boys and girls and men and women to join My army.*

*When you join, I will write your name in the Book of Life. You can serve with Me forever. I'll be waiting to hear from you.*

*Your Commander in Chief,*

*Jesus*

## PROCEDURE

Many years ago, young men 18 years and older received a letter in their mailbox. They were being "drafted" (called by the government to serve in the United States Army). This is a different type of "draft" letter, one that you'll be glad to receive. It's from the Voluntary Draft Board of Heaven. *(Open the letter and read it to the kids.)*

This is a voluntary draft letter asking for men, women, boys and girls to join God's army. We sign up on our knees in prayer. We are to ask Jesus for help. He will show us the way. Actually we are giving our lives—probably not in death, but we give up our lives of sin and trade them for lives of righteousness. Righteousness is doing what is right.

Everyone is invited to be a part of the greatest army ever assembled. There are special jobs for everyone to fill, so sign up and get ready to serve.

## PROCEDURE

### Purified

**The Point:** Jesus cleans us up on the inside.

**Props:** Chlorine, large clear bowl filled with water to which red food coloring has been added.

Look at this bowl of red water. It is like a life that has been colored by sin. It is no longer clear and pure. We know we've been called to live lives of purity. But, hey...what are we going to do? This water is already red, so there's really nothing we can we do about it, right? Wrong!

*(Pour chlorine into the red water. It will turn clear.)*

Whoa! What happened? The water isn't red anymore. It's been purified because we added chlorine to the water.

That's what happens when we ask Jesus into our lives. He comes in and cleans up on the inside. Once He lives within us, any time we are tempted to do wrong and lose our purity, we can call on Him to help us be faithful to His Word.

## The Everlasting Promise

**The Point:** Our relationship with Jesus lasts forever.

**Props:** Clear overhead transparency, permanent marker and erasable marker. Note: Make sure the ink from the erasable marker is easily removed.

### PROCEDURE

All of us have friends. *(Write "friends" with the erasable marker on the transparency.)* They are an important part of our lives and can even seem to be the most important at times. Well, the reality of those friendships is that one day we'll grow up. Changes take place in our lives and in our friends' lives, too. The friends we have today could one day move away. We may lose contact with them. (Wipe "friends" off the transparency.)

How about parents? A close relationship with our parents is something that is meant to last a long time. *(Write "parents" on the transparency.)* Each one of you is growing, and one day you'll move away from home. You'll get married and have a family of your own. You'll still have your parents, but your relationship with them will change as you get older. *(Wipe "parents" from the transparency.)*

Let's think of other relationships we can list. *(Allow for responses.)* Let's include "teachers," "pets" and "relatives." *(Continue to list the responses, and discuss how the relationships will pass. Then erase them from the transparency.)* All of these relationships will come and go. One relationship comes with a promise.

*(Use the permanent marker to write "Jesus" on the transparency.)* It's a promise we can count on. Jesus said He would never leave us or forsake us. He said He would be with us always. That's something that I can count on, no matter what happens in my life. *(Try to wipe off "Jesus.")*

Jesus and His promises for my life are not going away. It's the same for you when you make Jesus the Lord of your life. You'll have good times and bad times, but no matter what happens, Jesus Christ will be there for you.

**The Point:** Love the Lord with all your strength.

**Props:** Large nail (or railroad spike).

## PROCEDURE

**W**hy do we love God? That's a good question, and the Bible has the answer. 1 John 4:19 says, "We love God because He first loved us." And how much does Jesus love us? He loves us with all His strength.

How can I prove that? Just think of all the strength Jesus has. As the Son of God, He can do anything. Do you think He had enough strength to stop those Roman soldiers from driving spikes through His hands and feet? Absolutely! *(Hold up nail.)* But instead of using His strength to destroy His enemies, Jesus used His strength to keep loving them. Wow! He did that both for them and for you, so He could die for their sins and yours.

Instead of using His strength to stop the soldiers from beating Him with a whip, He used His strength to let them beat Him. Why? Because He loved you so much He wanted to take the beating you deserved. Instead of using His strength to get revenge when they laughed at Him, spit at Him and yanked out His beard, He used it to say, "Father, forgive them." And He gives us His forgiveness, too. Instead of using His strength to avoid being crucified, He used it to be obedient to God. And God raised him from the dead. Why? So you and I could live forever, too.

Since Jesus loved us with all His strength, will you love Him with all your strength? How can you use all your physical strength to love God? How about these ways:

- Use the strength in your legs and feet to go only to those places He wants you to go. *(Have the kids stand up.)*

- Use the strength in your hands and arm to serve God and others. *(Have kids lift their hands.)*

- Use the strength in your mouth to say things that bless God and others. *(Have them shout, "Praise the Lord!")*

- If you will love the Lord with all your strength, turn around three times, then sit down!

You really can love God with all your strength, but only because He loved you first. Let Him fill you with His love.

## PREPARATION

**B**efore the service starts, put a few drops of blue food coloring in the first glass. Put a few drops of red food coloring in the second glass. The third glass remains empty.

## PROCEDURE

*Pour water into first glass with blue food coloring.)* Sin causes our lives to be dark and ugly. Because of sin, our soul is full of guilt and hurt. We need someone to forgive us. Forgiveness can happen only through the blood of Christ.

*(Pour water into second glass with red food coloring.)* Christ paid the penalty for our sins so we could receive forgiveness. The penalty He paid was death on a cross.

*(Pour water into third glass.)* The result of Christ's dying for us is God's forgiveness. We can be clean and pure inside. To receive His forgiveness, we must admit we are sinners *(point to first glass)*, believe Jesus died for us *(point to second glass)* and ask Him to forgive us *(point to last glass)*.

## How Jesus Forgives Us

**The Point:** The blood of Jesus washes away our sin.

**Props:** Pitcher of water, three glasses, blue and red food coloring.

## How Jesus' Blood Changes Us

**The Point:** We are new people in Christ.

**Props:** Blank transparency, pictures of caterpillar, cocoon and butterfly

### PREPARATION

**M**ake a transparency using the pictures of a caterpillar, a cocoon and a butterfly.

### PROCEDURE

*(Show picture of caterpillar. Keep the rest of the transparency covered.)* Look at this caterpillar. It's not exactly pretty. Your life is just like this caterpillar when sin is in it—it's ugly. But then something happens to this caterpillar. It is hidden inside a cocoon.

(Show the picture of the cocoon.) The ugliness is hidden, just as our sins are hidden in Christ when we accept His forgiveness. But Christ doesn't just hide our sin; He actually changes us.

(Show the butterfly.) It's a miracle! The caterpillar becomes a butterfly. But it's a much greater miracle when Christ changes us from sinners into Christians.

The caterpillar can only inch along, but the butterfly can soar. As sinners we can only inch along in guilt and fear, but as new people in Christ, we will one day be able to soar to heaven!

## PROCEDURE

### The Apple Seed

**The Point:** God cares more about what's in our hearts than the size of our offerings.

**Props:** Apple, sharp knife and giving containers. (Suggested: baskets or gift boxes.)

**H**ow many of you have ever been apple picking? *(Show apple.)* How many of you know where apples come from? But where does the apple tree come from? Inside of each apple there is a core that holds a number of apple seeds. *(Take knife and cut apple in half. Find an apple seed and hold it up for kids to see.)*

This seed is quite small. Yet, if just one of these seeds is planted and it receives the right amount of water, light and warmth, an apple tree will grow. After the tree is grown, a whole bushel of apples may be picked from that one tree. That seed doesn't seem like much, but in the right circumstances it will bear a lot of fruit. It actually multiplies itself many times.

In the same way, sometimes you may think you don't have much to give to God. Yet God can take the little bit you have and multiply it.

Maybe you only have a small tithe or offering. God understands. The most important thing is not the size of it, but that you give it to God. When you give to God, He will take your offering and multiply it, just like an apple seed.

## PREPARATION

**H**ave helper inside box. Give helper the large shoe, fork, ball and dollar bill.

## PROCEDURE

### God's Return Box

**The Point:** We cannot out-give God.

**Props:** Refrigerator box (or curtain, puppet stage, etc.), small shoe, matching large shoe, small fork, large fork, small ball, giant-sized ball, dollar bill and giant-sized dollar bill (this can be a drawing).

I'm sure you've noticed something different on the platform. This box is a special invention that is based on a biblical principle. God shows us that when we give to Him, He will bless us and give back to us even more than we gave to Him (Mal. 3:10-11).

Watch this! *(Drop the small fork in the box. The helper throws the large fork out of the box.)* Wow! See this? When you put in something small, it increases!

*(Place ball in box. Large one is thrown out of box.)* Isn't this incredible? *(Put shoe in box. Large one is thrown out.)* Wow! Whatever is put in comes back larger, just as God's Word promises us when we give to Him!

When we give our talents to the Lord, He can take that talent and help us increase it. When we give some of our time to the Lord as we read our Bibles and pray, God will bless us for it!

Malachi 3:10 and 11 states that when we give the Lord our tithes and offerings, *(put small bill in)* He will open the windows of heaven and pour out more blessings than we have room for. So even if you feel you don't have much to give to God, give it anyway. *(Pull out large bill.)* He will take that little bit and increase it.

Let's give to God our time, tithes, talents and gifts today.

## Rich Young Ruler

**The Point:** God wants to control every aspect of our lives.

**Props:** Large poster and marker.

### PREPARATION

**H**ave the drawing pre-done and hold the poster at this time, or begin the drawing of a face that is smiling when held upright and frowning when upside down. See example below.

### PROCEDURE

In Matthew 19:20-21, we read about a young man who talked with Jesus. This young man asked Jesus, "Teacher, what good thing must I do to get eternal life?"

Jesus and the young man talked for a while, then at the end of their conversation Jesus told him, "Go, sell your possessions and give to the poor, and you will have treasure in heaven. Then come, follow me."

This young man was quite wealthy. He owned many nice things. He also had followed the Ten Commandments and acted the way God had instructed. But Jesus knew there was one thing that would stand between God and that young man.

The man loved the things he owned even more than he loved God. Evidently Jesus wanted him to become a disciple. But the man became sad, and he went away. *(Turn picture upside down so face is now frowning.)*

When we talk about giving the Lord our entire lives, that includes our money. God has blessed us in many ways. The least we can do is give our tithes back to Him. Some people today are like that rich young man; they want to follow Jesus, but they're not willing to give Jesus control of everything. Let's allow God to use our talents, our time and our money. You'll find that's when you will have true happiness. *(Turn picture right side up again.)* Let's give to God today our time, talents and the amount of money that pleases Him. *(Receive the boys' and girls' offering for the Lord. Ask a boy or girl to pray over the gifts given today.)*

## PROCEDURE

**The Point:** Your offering helps bring the gospel to others.

**Props:** Plastic pipe (2- to 5-foot section) and two or three marbles. Write "you" on pipe.

**S**ome have never heard about Jesus. (*Select a boy and girl. Have the girl stand to your left, the boy to your right. Hold marbles.*) We will have the boy represent one who has never heard the Good News, and the girl will represent a Christian. She has received the Good News. (*Hand the marbles to her.*) These are the Good News marbles. (*Pick up the pipe.*)

She has a problem. She knows that God desires that all people come to know Him, but she can't get the Good News to the boy. She can't walk over to him. She can't throw or roll the marbles to him.

(*Hold the pipe horizontally between the children.*) But there's one thing she can do. She can use this pipe to send the Good News marbles to him. (*Allow her to place marbles in pipe. Let them roll out the other end for the boy to catch.*)

In the same way, God wants to send the Good News of His love to everyone. He wants to use you (*show "you" on pipe*) to get the Good News out to others.

We should share the message of Jesus with people all around us. But what about people in other countries? Obviously, we cannot all go to Africa. But we all can give offerings that will help others to go. God will use your offerings to help pay for a "pipeline" so that the Good News can get from where we are (*point to girl*) out to those who need Christ (*point to boy*).

So allow God to use you—your talents and your tithes—to help send the gospel out to the world around you.

## PROCEDURE

### Give It Back to Whom It Belongs

**The Point:** Give to God what belongs to Him.

**Props:** Assorted U.S. coins.

Kids, did you bring your offering today? I want you to pull out the coins or bills because we're going to look at something special on each of these.

Have you noticed that on each of these pieces of money there is a picture of someone?

Whose picture is on a penny? *Lincoln's.* Whose picture is on a nickel? *Jefferson's.* Whose picture is on a dime? *Roosevelt's.* Whose picture is on a quarter? *Washington's.*

What did all of these men have in common? They were Presidents of the United States. On each of your coins it even says, "The United States of America." It lets us know where this money is from.

Jesus was asked about whether or not He should give money to the government. He told them to bring Him a coin. Then He asked them, "Whose picture is on this?" They replied that it was Caesar. You see, Caesar was the ruler of the country at that time.

Jesus said, "Well then, give to Caesar what belongs to Caesar, and give to God what belongs to God." Look at your offering again. Something else is written on the money. It says, "In God We Trust."

Jesus said we should give to God what belongs to Him. Right here on our money it says that we trust God. If we really do trust Him, we will trust Him with our money, too.

*(Have one of your boys or girls pray over your offering and receive the tithes, gifts and offerings from the kids.)*

## PROCEDURE

**The Point:** We need to use our time and talents to help others know God.

**Props:** Chalkboard (or large tablet on easel).

**D**o you know that God has given each of us talents? Yes, He has, but what is a talent? A talent is something that you can do well. Here are some of the talents God has given to me: *(List some of your talents on the chalkboard.)* God has given all of us things that we can do well.

Think of some talents God has given you. Your talent may be that you run fast, can sing, play an instrument or are a good actor. You may be good at helping to care for babies or growing plants in a garden. *(Ask kids to share their answers. As they do, write them on the board.)*

Do you know why God has given us talents? *(Let them give a few answers.)* God wants us to use them for Him. You could write a poem about God's love and read it, or sing a song in church for Jesus. That would be using your talents for God. How could you use some of the talents listed here to serve the Lord? *(Ask for a response.)*

God wants us to give our time and talents to Him, as well as our money. Our money is important, and it is used to help tell others about Jesus. But we need to use our time and talents to help others to know about Him. As we give our offerings of money today, let's think of ways to use our talents for God also.

## PROCEDURE

### First Fruits

**The Point:** We should always give our best to God.

**Props:** Good apple and rotten apple, (or good and bad piece of any fruit).

God wants our very best. God does not want us to bring Him our leftovers. When we finish eating at our house, we give the scraps to the dogs. It wouldn't be very nice of us to treat God like one of our dogs and say, "I'm through eating. Here, You can have the rest." That's not what we'd do if company came to our house, and it shouldn't be the way we treat God.

*(Hold up the two apples.)* Which one of these should we give as a gift to God? Yes, of course we should give Him the best.

The Bible tells us to give God the first fruits of the harvest, not the leftovers. Let's be sure we're really giving our best to God. He deserves nothing less than that. God says we are a precious treasure to Him. God wants to be a precious treasure to us, so let's give Him the best of what we have. If we give Him our best, He will give us His best.

## God Blesses Our Little

**The Point:** God can multiply our offering, no matter how small.

**Props:** Air popcorn popper, bowl and popcorn.

### PROCEDURE

Sometimes when you bring your offering and it is not very much, you may wonder how this helps the church at all. It's just too little. You wish you could give a lot. It's nice of you to want to give more to Jesus, but God wants just what you can give Him, and then He'll take it and multiply it. Think of the story of how Jesus fed the 5,000.

Let's say today that each of you brought just one kernel of popcorn. That would not look like much. *(Hold out a handful of popcorn kernels.)* But take that and put it in the Master's hand! Think of the air popper as being the Master's hand today. We'll see what happens when we put this small amount of popcorn in it. *(Turn it on and let it pop the corn while you take the offering. Show them how much popcorn you have now.)* It didn't look like much when we started, but now we have a great big bowl of popcorn!

When we give to God, it doesn't matter if it's just a small amount. God can multiply what we give. If we are obedient in giving, God will bless us.

## PROCEDURE

**Phone Call From God**

**The Point:** We can show God we love Him by giving our offerings.

**Props:** Phone.

**W**ell what should we do next? *(Make the sound of a phone ringing.)* Oh, I wonder who's calling us? *(Answer with a surprised look.)* Oh...hi, God! What? You're calling to see if we remembered You this morning? Well, I thought about You. *(Ask the kids if they thought about God.)* Yes! How did we show that we thought about You? That's a good question, God. *(Hold hand over receiver.)* I wonder, kids, how could we have shown God this morning that we haven't forgotten Him? In fact, how could we show Him that we were thinking about Him? I know, we could have brought an offering!

*(Get back on phone.)* You think about us all the time, don't you, God? Yes, we know You want us to think about You often and show You we love You. We're doing that right now. *(Hold up phone to group.)* OK, let's tell God we love Him. *(Have them repeat it. Hang up phone.)* This morning as we give our offering, let's think about God and how much He loves us. And let's think about ways we can show Him that we think about Him and love Him.

## The "I"-itis Disease

**The Point:** Let's get our eyes on Jesus and off ourselves.

**Props:** Two 1- by 4-foot pieces of white posterboard, one 2- by 4-foot piece of white posterboard, tape, chalkboard and chalk.

## PREPARATION

Make an "I" with the three pieces of posterboard. Let them lean against a chalkboard for support. Apply rolled up tape to back of pieces to secure them. (See diagram below.)

## PROCEDURE

Have you ever been sick? It's not very much fun to be sick. It's more fun to be well so you can go outside, play with your friends or ride your bike. Have you ever known anyone who was very sick? I just heard about a terrible disease. It is hard to cure. You may know someone who has it. This disease is called "I"-itis. Ever hear of it? You catch it when you stop caring about other people and care only about yourself.

"I"-itis is difficult to cure. You can always recognize someone who has the disease by listening to how they talk. You will hear the word "I" a lot! I want! I need! I can't! I don't! I won't! People with this disease have a hard time giving friendship to others or giving love to God. All they care about is numero uno.

There is a cure for "I"-itis. It's not found in a bottle of aspirin. *(Rearrange the posterboard to make a cross. Apply rolled up tape to back of pieces to secure them.)* If we think about Jesus and what He did for us on the cross, "I"-itis will go away, because you can't think about yourself when you think about Jesus.

The cross you see has two parts. The first section is a vertical line which points us to God. It connects heaven and earth. It reminds us that God in heaven sent Jesus to this sinful earth to be a sacrifice for our sin. The second section is the horizontal line. This line reminds us that Jesus reaches out to everyone with His love. Today, as you are giving your tithes and offerings to God, think about His love. Let's keep our eyes on Jesus and not on ourselves.

## PROCEDURE

**Circle of Protection**

**The Point:** We can trust that God will protect us.

**Props:** None.

I need some volunteers! *(Choose a group of children and have them form a "Circle of Protection" around you as you speak.)* Obedience to God and worship puts you in a supernatural place. The Bible says in Psalm 23 that even though "I walk through the valley of the shadow of death, I don't need to fear evil." Trouble can be all around. People can say bad things about you, but God will protect you.

But sin and disobedience can cause a gap in the circle of protection. *(Have kids in the circle join hands. Appoint a helper on the outside of the circle to try [unsuccessfully] to break through.)* Doubting God's ability to help you or grumbling and complaining can cause a break. We should build up one another with good speech and thoughts. *(Have the kids break hands at one point so the helper can join in the circle.)*

Don't let bad thoughts stay in your mind or let unpleasant words come out of your mouth. The angels forming the "Circle of Protection" will not stay around to listen to that kind of thing. But God's angels are servants to the children of God, and it is their job to keep you safe from harm and danger in the "Circle of Protection."

## PROCEDURE

### Pizza Faith

**The Point:** God always keeps His promises.

**Props:** Pizza delivery box and telephone.

**H**ow many of you like pizza? *(Pick up pizza box.)* How many of you like sausage pizza? pepperoni pizza? taco pizza? peanut butter pizza? *(Put down pizza box.)*

All right, let's say you go home from church today and decide to order a pizza. You pick up the telephone *(pick up receiver)* and dial the number of your favorite pizza delivery place.

(Wait as if telephone is ringing, then speak into the receiver.) Hello. Yes, I'd like to order a large pizza with everything on it...yes, with purple onions, too. That's fine. Yes, my address is 137 Pine Street. Thank you. *(Hang up the telephone.)*

Now tell me, how do you know the pizza-man is going to deliver pizza to you? *Because he said he would.*

You say this pizza place delivers whenever they say they will. But how do you know you can trust them this time?

Well, you really don't know. You have to decide you will trust them to bring the pizza. That's what faith is: deciding you will trust someone or something.

We can place our faith in God because He always keeps His promises. He has never broken a promise that He's made. His Word is true, and He always delivers what He says He will.

## A Heart Full

### PREPARATION

Cut out a large heart from red posterboard. (The heart should be large enough for all of the kids to see.) Secure an additional piece of posterboard on the back of the heart so it can stand on a table. Behind the heart (where the kids cannot see) have a teen fashion magazine, video game and Walkman®.

**The Point:** God's word helps us to live right.

**Props:** Red posterboard, tape (or glue), teen fashion magazines, video game, Walkman® and Bible.

### PROCEDURE

The Bible says we should hide God's Word in our heart. *(Hold up the Bible for the kids to see.)* How can we do that? There's no way I can get this Bible in this heart! *(Act like you are trying to cram the Bible into your heart.)* So how do you get God's Word in your heart? You read it. You go to church and learn what's in it. You memorize it. That takes time, lots of time. But it's worth it. When you have God's Word in your heart, the Holy Spirit will remind you of this verse or that verse—exactly when you need it.

What do you have hidden in your heart? Let's see what's hiding in this one. *(From behind the heart, lift up a fashion magazine.)* Looks like we have a magazine. *(Scan through it.)* What's in! What's out! That's good to know. What else? Here's a video game. *(Show game.)* Those are fun. And a Walkman®. *(Show Walkman®.)* No kid should be without one of these, right?

What if you're going through a tough time in school or at home, or both? You're all mixed up and you don't know what you're supposed to do. You need some answers. Is it going to do any good to know the top ten hits on the pop chart? What if your best friend comes to you and wants to know how to be saved? Is it going to help to tell him what the "in" hairstyle is? None of these things are bad, but don't let them take all your time. Leave room in your heart for God's Word. Take time to read your Bible.

## PROCEDURE

**Feeding on God's Word**

**The Point:** God's word makes us healthy and able to resist sin.

**Props:** Two mixing bowls, spoon, various ingredients (milk, sugar, baking powder, salt, etc.) and Bible.

**A**s you know, what you put inside your body is very important. (*Add whatever ingredients you have into the first bowl and stir them as you talk.*) If we are going to be healthy, feel good and have strength and energy, we must eat healthy foods. Sometimes children die of malnutrition because of a lack of healthy nourishing food in their diet.

But do you know what is more sad than dying of starvation or malnutrition? It is people who have not taken any of God's Word into their body. (*Put the Bible into the second bowl.*)

You may be wondering, "How do you eat God's Word?'" Every time you read it, it goes into your body through your eyes. Every time you listen to the Bible being read, it goes in through your ears. When you speak memory verses, the Bible also goes in through your ears and into your body. It doesn't just go to your brain, as other words in books do. It goes right down into the inside of your bones, into the marrow. It adds bone marrow to you, and it also adds moisture to your bones. It is like putting medicine on your flesh when you read it or take it in.

When God's Word goes inside of us, it builds up an immunity or a protection against sin. Good health repels sickness. When you are strong and healthy, it is hard to get sick. When you have God's Word, you are not attracted to sin. It becomes ugly and nasty and you want to stay away from it.

Every day make sure you get some of the Word inside of you, not just your normal food. In the Bible, Job said God's Word is even more important than our regular body food. It will make us strong against the sin that makes the body weak.

## The Key of Truth

**The Point:** Truth unlocks the door to righteous living.

**Props:** Large chain (or rope) padlock and four keys. (Only one key should fit the padlock.)

### PREPARATION

Label the correct key for the lock, "Jesus" on one side and "Truth" on the other. Label the other three keys, "Money," "Popularity" and "Ability." Have one child come forward and bind him with the chains.

### PROCEDURE

We want to live holy lives, so it is important to be like Jesus and to always be truthful. Jesus said, "I am the way, the TRUTH, and the life." Truth is a key to freedom. *(Hold up "freedom" padlock and key.)* When we lie, one lie leads to another and soon we are tangled in a web of deceit. Jesus said "You will know the truth and the truth will make you free." Truth is a key that unlocks the way to understanding. Lies can never bring understanding, for they are shaky, wobbly and always changing. Truth does not change. Truth is holy, and like God, it never changes.

You see, we can try to get free with money, popularity or athletic ability, but none of those keys will do the trick. *(Try to unlock the padlock with the "false" keys.)* The only key that frees us from the bondage of sin is the absolute truth of God's Word, and that truth is Jesus. *(Unlock the padlock and set the child free.)*

**God's Word**

## PROCEDURE

**Refreshments**

**The Point:** God's refreshing word gives us strength to do right.

**Props:** Can of soda and glass of ice.

Boy, on a hot day after a long game of basketball or baseball, what is the first thing you want? (*Open the can of soda while you are speaking.*) Do you want a cup of hot coffee? How about hot chocolate? No, what you want is something cold to drink, right? (*Pour can of soda into glass.*) When you take that drink after a long game, it tastes really good, doesn't it? (*Take a drink.*) Sure tastes good.

Why does it taste so good? Why wouldn't coffee or hot chocolate be good? (*Take a few answers.*) Coffee or hot chocolate wouldn't hit the spot because they aren't refreshing. When you're hot, you want something cold to drink. Only a cold drink will be refreshing.

The Bible is like drinking this cold soda. It's meant to refresh you in the things of God. When you read the Bible, you get fired up again about obeying Jesus. You get filled up with good teaching. (*Take a drink.*) After a hard day of fighting the enemy and enduring trials, God's Word refreshes you. How does the Bible refresh you? By filling you with God's way of thinking. By giving you strength and power to live right. Kids, let's be thankful for God's precious Word.

## PREPARATION

**M**ake directional signs out of cardboard. Set up the signs in front of the room. Pin up the map on a bulletin board.

## PROCEDURE

### Direction Signs

**The Point:** Going to church helps us see God's direction.

**Props:** Large city map, directional signs (stop, yield, and caution).

One reason people go to gas stations is to get directions. When they are lost, people usually pull into a gas station to ask for directions to their destination. They might have passed their exit or gotten off at the wrong exit. Your church helps you grow as a Christian by providing direction.

At church, you find out the way to go to heaven, and you learn how to please God. There might be something in your life that you're doing wrong. You might not know this until you go to church. Then you learn that you need to stop *(point to stop sign)* doing it. Or you might be doing something that you need to be careful about. At church you learn *(point to caution sign)* caution. You also learn to *(point to yield sign)* yield to God. We need to be thankful for our church because it provides direction.

**God's Word**

## PROCEDURE

**The Point:** We should be proud of God's Word.

**Props:** Large Bible (the largest you can find) and small New Testament.

The Bible is the Word of God. *(Pause.)* I said that the Bible is the Word of God. *(Pause.)* Let me put it another way: The Bible is God's Word. It is God speaking to us! When I think about that, it amazes me that we don't spend more time reading what God has to say to us.

Not only do we not spend enough time reading it, but some church kids even seem ashamed of the Word of God. They don't want their non-Christian friends to know they believe in the Bible.

When I was younger, I decided I was going to take my Bible every place I went. I said, "If they don't like my Bible around, then I don't want to be around that place." For a long time that's the way I lived. I carried my Bible everywhere.

*(Display the large Bible.)* How would you feel about taking a Bible like this to school? Would it embarrass you? God's Word is more important than all your school books put together. Are you proud of it? God's Word can change your life, make you joyful and lead you to heaven. Do you want other people to know that?

You probably wouldn't be embarrassed to take this big Bible with you to church. You might even be proud of it, thinking it makes you look like a good Christian. Yes, it's easy to want to look like a good person, to look like a real Christian, when you're at church. But do you feel the same way when you're at school, at home and in your neighborhood?

Well, I'm not saying you have to carry along a two-ton Bible to be a true Christian. *(Put down the large Bible.)* But you must not be ashamed of God and His Word. *(Pick up the small New Testament.)* I do think if you begin to carry a Bible, like this small New Testament, with you and let people know what you believe in, you will see goodness grow in your life. Because of your bold stand, the Holy Spirit will grow goodness and other fruit of the Spirit in you.

Why don't you make up your mind to not go anywhere your Bible would not be welcome? Then be proud of God's Word wherever you go!

## PROCEDURE

**Diet for Success**

**The Point:** God has a recipe for a healthy spiritual diet.

**Props:** Mixing bowl, apron, large spoon and small boxes (or cans) wrapped in plain paper and labeled: Faith, Worship, Church Attendance, Bible Reading, Prayer, Money, Alarm Clock.

I have a recipe to whip up for us today. This is a recipe for living a healthy Christian life. *(Stir as you talk.)* First, I am going to put Church Attendance in the mixing bowl. *(Hold up can labeled "Church Attendance.")* This is where we learn to worship God. *(Hold up can labeled "Worship.")* Worship and church attendance mixed together create a desire to read the Bible. *(Hold up can labeled "Bible Reading.")* The Bible causes faith to grow inside of you. *(Hold up can labeled "Faith.")*

If I were baking cookies or a cake, I would add eggs to hold everything together. I would add baking power to make it rise. We must not leave anything out of this spiritual recipe if we want it to turn out right.

Now we add prayer. *(Hold up can labeled "Prayer.")* Giving is an important part, too. I will put money in *(hold up can labeled "Money")* and also add an alarm clock. *(Hold up can labeled "Alarm Clock.")* We need to give God some of our time.

Yum, yum! No need for a stove, just mixing this spiritual recipe together will make you strong in your spirit.

This recipe is a promise that if you mix all these together, you will have a nutritional diet that will help you grow in your spirit.

## It Lights

**The Point:** The Holy Spirit makes our lights bright for Christ.

**Props:** Flashlight without the batteries inserted, the batteries in plain view, extension cord and tools.

## PROCEDURE

This flashlight just won't come on! *(This is to be somewhat comical, so have fun with it. The idea here is that your flashlight won't work. It has a good bulb, so it should work. Try to get the light to light by doing everything but putting in the batteries. Turn it on, turn it upside down, twist it, shake it, stand on one foot, hold your mouth funny.)*

Oh, it needs power. *(Hook it up to the extension cord. Try to fix it with the tools. Finally, when you have had enough of the kids yelling at you to put the batteries in the flashlight, do so and make it light.)*

When batteries are put in a flashlight, it lights. Jesus said that we are the light of the world. But our own lights aren't very bright. The power of the Holy Spirit is the only power that can really make our lights bright. Our lights become more effective for Jesus when we receive the power of the Holy Spirit. His power gives us the power to share the love of Jesus with others in a brighter way. Peter became a powerful light showing people the way to follow Jesus.

## Apple Power

**The Point:** The Holy Spirit brings power.

**Props:** Apple and knife.

### PROCEDURE

I like apples! Apple pie, apple crisp, apple fritters, mmmm good!

Inside this apple is a secret power. You can't see the power by looking at the outside of the apple, but it is there. It is a power to do some incredible things. Let's look deep inside this apple and see if we can see this apple's secret power *(Slice the apple in half and pick some seeds out.)* There it is, so small but so powerful: A seed, yes, a seed. In this little tiny seed is the power to grow not just another apple but a whole tree covered with apples.

God has something powerful for us that we can't see. God's secret power for us is His Holy Spirit. God wants us to be filled with this power. His power can't be seen, but it is still there. When we are filled with this power, we have a secret weapon deep inside us to use for God.

When we are filled with this secret weapon, we have the power to stand up for Jesus, power to do His will and power to defeat the devil.

## PROCEDURE

### Prisoners

**The Point:** God's Holy Spirit will enable us.

**Props:** Ropes (or clothesline), chains (can be plastic or paper) boy or girl prisoner, two men and a chair.

Sometimes men are captured by the enemy and thrown into a concentration camp. (*Have your prisoner brought in and tie him or her in the chair as you speak.*) Cruel stories have been told of the torture of prisoners in order to get secrets and knowledge from them. (*Look at your prisoner.*)

The Christian soldier's enemy, the devil, made a big mistake. He didn't know what he was doing when he gave evil men the idea to kill Jesus. Jesus went to His Father in heaven after the crucifixion and He sent the secret weapon to earth to be used in the lives of every soldier in God's army.

(*Act as if you are trying to get the chained prisoner to talk.*) "Tell us, is it money that makes you so powerful?" (*Prisoner shakes head no.*) "Is it a lucky charm that gives you your power?" *No!* "Do you live by the stars?" *No!* "Is there a safe where this secret is kept?" *No!* "Is it in a secret code?" *No!* "Tell us, tell us. What is the secret of your power, your happiness, joy, health and success?"

(*Prison rips off the ropes and becomes a witness.*) He yells out, "The Holy Spirit is my secret weapon."

WOW! I guess so. GO! You're free. (*Thank your prisoner for helping you with this object lesson and explain to the kids that with the Holy Spirit in your life you have more power than any of your enemies.*)

## Pearl of Great Price

**The Point:** We can become like beautiful pearls in the hands of God.

**Props:** Real (or fake) pearl and bowl of sand (or salt).

## PROCEDURE

**H**ow many of you know how a pearl is made? *(Hold up pearl.)* For those of you who don't know, a pearl is made by the oyster when a grain of sand gets into its shell. The oyster keeps coating the grain of sand until someone finds the oyster, opens it up and finds the oyster's precious gift—the pearl.

We're like this pearl. God takes what we are and gives us everything we need to become a beautiful gift for Him.

If we don't use the time, money and talent God has given us by giving it back to Him, we can never develop into the beautiful and wonderful gift God intended. We'll just be grains of sand. *(Let some sand sift through your fingers.)* But if we use what God has given us properly, when He looks inside us God will see a precious gift—you and me. Which would you rather be, a small grain of sand or a beautiful pearl?

## The Pickpocket

**The Point:** If we keep our focus on Jesus, the enemy won't defeat us.

**Props:** Large wallet and three helpers: pickpocket, decoy and victim.

### PROCEDURE

The devil wants to rip us off. *(Have victim leave wallet sticking out of his pocket. The decoy bumps into the victim and engages him in conversation while the pickpocket steals the wallet. You are talking as the skit progresses.)*

He wants to steal our joy, happiness, peace and walk with God. Just as the decoy distracts the victim for the pickpocket, Satan distracts us many times through our families. By getting us to focus on problems in our family, he is able to steal our relationship with God. Don't be distracted by his tricks! Don't let him get you to focus on your family's problems! No family is perfect. Keep your focus on God, and try to keep your family's focus on God. Looking to Jesus, the one who started and the one who will bring our faith to maturity, is the key to defeating Satan and his tricks. Even if your family is having difficulty, you can have peace and joy in the midst of the trouble by keeping your eyes on Jesus. And you can stand strong for your family in prayer and ask God to heal it.

## PREPARATION

**C**olor one piece of paper with fresh "wet" paint.

## PROCEDURE

### Rubbed the Wrong Way

**The Point:** We will become like those we hang out with.

**Props:** Two pieces paper and paint (or mud or lead pencil).

Watch what happens when I put this clean piece of paper against this dirty piece of paper. Does the dirty one get clean? No! Does the clean one get dirty? Yes! If you spend time with people who cause trouble, guess what happens to you? That's right, the messes they get into slop on you. You'll get the blame for things you might have had no hand in doing. But because you hang out with those who are getting dirty, you'll look dirty to a lot of people. Eventually, rubbing up against those who steal can lead you into stealing. Not only will your relationship with friends and family who stay clean be muddied, your relationship with God will, too. That's why we need to stay close to Jesus. The Bible says that if we do, we'll be continually cleaned up by His blood.

## PROCEDURE

**The Point:** God rewards faithfulness.

**Props:** Paycheck (or copy of paycheck).

At the end of every week, I get one of these. *(Show your paycheck.)* I get this paycheck for one reason—because I faithfully do my job. I am paid for the work I do. *(Tell the kids about your job. Explain your responsibilities.)*

What would happen if I went to work tomorrow and told my boss, "I quit!" Would I get a paycheck on Friday? Of course not! I have to be faithful to my job if I want to get paid.

God has a job for me to do as well. The job He has is for me to serve Him faithfully. I do this by praying faithfully, reading God's Word faithfully, giving offerings faithfully, obeying God faithfully and teaching you faithfully. If I continue to be faithful to Him, one day He will reward me. But my reward won't be a paycheck like this one. It will be much greater! When I go to heaven, God will tell me, "Well done, good and faithful servant." Then He'll give me rewards that will last forever.

That day may seem a long time off, but that doesn't matter. As Paul said, I am going to try as hard as I can to reach the goal that is set before me. That goal is heaven and God's rewards. With His help, I am going to reach that goal. How about you?

## PREPARATION

rite the word "Hello" on the posterboard.

## PROCEDURE

### Little Acts

**The Point:** When we're kind to others, we show God's love.

**Props:** Cookies, dish detergent and posterboard.

Showing kindness to others doesn't mean we always have to do big things for them. In fact, most kind acts are small deeds done out of love. Here are a few examples.

*(Show the cookies.)* Suppose you were eating lunch with some kids, and you pulled out this bag of cookies from your lunch box. You could show kindness by simply sharing the cookies.

*(Display the dish detergent.)* How could you use this stuff in an act of kindness? Of course! You could do your mom or dad a favor by washing the dishes without being asked. Or when you are asked to wash the dishes, you could do so without complaining about it. That would be acting in kindness.

*(Show the sign.)* Hello! Kindness can sometimes be nothing more than just saying hello to someone. Maybe there is someone at church or school whom no one talks to very much. Perhaps the kindest thing you could do for that person would be talk with him.

How many of you could share a snack, do a chore around the house, or speak to someone who's alone? Each of you could!

I realize that all of us have those times when we don't feel like being kind. We don't want to go to the trouble of treating others the way we should. In those times, we should ask the Holy Spirit to change our hearts. We should ask Him to give us the fruit of kindness. He will! He is the source of true kindness.

## PREPARATION

### The Right Stuff

**The Point:** The Spirit of God gives us self-control.

**Props:** Blank transparency and transparency marker.

**W**rite the following list on a blank transparency:

- 7:15    Woke up late, so I didn't take time to pray.

- 7:30    Mom wasn't feeling well, so I fixed my own cereal.

- 8:30    A kid tripped me in the school hallway. I felt like hitting him, but I didn't.

- 10:00   My teacher left the room, so we all made fun of her.

- 11:00   Had a chance to cheat on my math test, but I didn't.

- 12:00   I goofed around so much at lunch that I didn't finish eating.

- 1:00    During gym I didn't hog the basketball.

- 2:00    I got in trouble for talking during reading time.

- 4:00    I did my homework before I went outside to play.

- 5:00    My mom said to stay on our block while I played. I obeyed her.

- 6:00    I teased my little sister at dinner.

- 8:00    Even though my mom was at the store, I didn't watch a program she had told me not to watch.

- 9:00    I prayed before I went to bed.

## PROCEDURE

This is a list of things Jason did one day. Follow along as I read it. *(Quickly read the list.)* In each situation, Jason faced the self-control issue. Would he and the Spirit of God be in control of his selfish self so he would do the right thing? Or would he let his fleshly (wrong) desires control him? *(For each item, have the kids tell you whether or not Jason acted with self-control. Put a check next to each item that shows self-control in action.)*

It is easy to know what Jason should have done in each of these situations, just as we usually know what we should do. However, it is another thing entirely to actually do what is right. That takes self-control. And having self-control takes the Spirit of God living within us along with our firm commitment to do what is right. *(Pray with your kids for self-control.)*

## Love

**The Point:** God is faithful to us even when don't deserve it.

**Props:** Three gift boxes (each with a single letter written on it: D-O-G). (Optional: Live dog.)

### PROCEDURE

Today we have some gifts that I want you to pay close attention to. As you can see, each one of these gifts has a letter written on it. Before you guess the word with these gifts, let me ask you some questions. How many of you have a pet?

How many of you have ever received a pet as a gift? *(Show gift boxes arranged in "D-O-G" order.)* Maybe some of you have received a dog as a present.

Often, after a person owns a dog for a while, the dog and its master really grow to love each other. Raise your hand if you have a dog you really love. Sometimes, even if the master is mean, the dog will remain faithful to him. Even if the owner doesn't feed the dog or take him for walks, often the dog will continue to love his owner.

The Bible talks about that idea when it talks about us and God. *(Rearrange blocks to spell "G-O-D.")* God loves us and remains faithful, even when we don't deserve it. Sometimes we don't show our love to God the way we should, but He still loves us. We should treat other people the same way. We should love them, whether they treat us well or not. Just as God loves us, we need to decide that we will love others. We may not feel they deserve it, but we still should give them the gift of love.

## Compassion

**The Point:** Compassion is seeing another person's need and doing something about it.

**Props:** Large puzzle (either a large cutout or a smaller puzzle on an overhead projector).

## PROCEDURE

Most people receive a variety of gifts at Christmas. One present you may have received is a puzzle. *(Work on the puzzle throughout this narration.)*

It's a fun and exciting challenge to figure out where puzzle pieces go. Some people accept the challenge and work hard at completing a puzzle. Others couldn't care less if a half-completed puzzle is ever finished.

I don't know if they had puzzles like this back in the days when Jesus walked on earth before His death and resurrection, but if they did, I think He would have been One who would work at the puzzle until it was completed.

You see, whenever Jesus saw there was an empty space—a real need—in a person's life, He'd do whatever He could to help fill that need. Jesus would fill in the missing pieces. If people had a space in their lives that needed healing, He would fill that space and heal them. When people were hungry and had nowhere to get food, He broke five loaves and two fish and fed more than 5,000 people.

That's just the way Jesus is. He loves people so much that if He sees some way He can help, He does. That's what compassion is—seeing a person's need, then doing something to help them out because of love. Jesus, when seeing a need, out of compassion just had to fill in the empty space.

Just as I filled in the empty spaces of our puzzle, Jesus wants us to help others fill in the spaces in their lives.

## PROCEDURE

### Strength in Friendship

**The Point:** We should pick friends who honor Jesus.

**Props:** Three volunteers and six 3-foot long pieces of string. The string should be thin enough that the kids can break it by pulling on it.

I need three strong volunteers. *(Have the three volunteers come forward. Give each a piece of string and ask him or her to break it. After they have done so, take the other three pieces of string and braid them together. Now have each child try to break the braided string. They can even join forces and take turns pulling on opposite ends. When it becomes evident that they cannot break the braided string, point out the importance of combined strength.)*

When I am alone, I can sometimes make big mistakes. I need friends who will help me stand firm. I want a friend who loves God more than anything else. I want a friend who will go to church with me, who doesn't lie, steal or cheat. I want a friend who honors his parents and respects others, a friend who honors Jesus at all times. That friend would help me to do the things I know are right, and I'd help my friend also. And, of course, the third member of our team would be God, who would help both of us. Together we'd be too strong to be broken! I need a friend like that, but most of all, I need to BE a friend like that.

## PROCEDURE

### C-H-R-I-S-T-I-A-N

**The Point:** Loving means accepting others' differences.

**Props:** Nine volunteers, and nine pieces of large posterboard with each letter of the word Christian written on a board.

**W**e're going to do something very special today. I'm going to test your spelling skills. *(Distribute the letters to your volunteers prior to doing the lesson. Be sure they are seated in different areas in the audience. As you lead the kids in saying each letter, have the child with that letter come up and stand in front of the room.)*

How many of you know how to spell the word Christian? OK, some of you need to come up here and remind me how to spell it. *(Have a few kids come up front.)*

What's the first letter? *(Have them answer.)* C. OK, C. The second letter? OK, h. *(Continue to do this until all the children with the letters are up front. Interrupt them a few times and ask if the whole word is spelled out.)*

Now what does this spell? Of course, Christian. You know what? It took nine people to come up and spell this word. Kids, what happens if I take off the n? What do we have? How about if I decide I don't like the s and take that out? Do I still have the word Christian. No? Why not? Right, because I don't have the n and the s.

We need all the letters to spell this word, right? Just as each letter is important to spell this word, so each one of you is important in expressing the fullness of Jesus Christ.

We may not like people because of their hair color, or maybe they don't dress right, but you know what? We still need them. We need each other. Kids, when you exclude somebody, you are closing a door that God may want to open. You are also not a very good example of showing Christ's love to others. Accepting one another is not an option. In fact, God commands us to love one another. Let's be like Jesus and love one another by accepting and including each other.

## The Sour Lemon Drink

**The Point:** What we do for Jesus will last forever.

**Props:** Lemon(s), pitcher of water, wastebasket and sugar. (Optional: Paper cups.)

### PROCEDURE

Some people use others like this lemon. They squeeze all they can out of others just to get what they can for themselves. *(Squeeze the lemon(s) into the pitcher of water as you are speaking.)* But in the end, they always end up bitter just like this juice because users are always losers. You see, Jesus said that only what we do for Him will really last. *(Toss the lemon rinds in the wastebasket.)*

But then there are others, true committed believers like *(name a strong Christian from your church the children will know)*. Did you ever notice they're always doing things for others? They're like this sugar. *(Pour the sugar into the lemon water.)* They bring the sweetness of God's love to a world that's gone sour.

The next time you're served a glass of lemonade, it might just be a little reminder from the Lord. Do a quick heart check. Are you a Christian gone sour, or one who is pouring the love of Jesus into all of the lives you touch?

## PREPARATION

Insert the $20 bill into the bag of cat litter prior to this lesson.

## PROCEDURE

### Surprise Inside

**The Point:** It is better to look for the value in others than judge by appearances.

**Props:** Bag of cat litter (or sand or dirt), three $1 dollar bills and one $20 bill (or play money).

OK, kids, we've got two prizes up here for the kid that has hair. Oh, that's right, you all have hair. *(Have a helper hold the bag of cat litter and another helper hold the three $1 bills in front of the room.)*

Anyway, I'm going to call one of you up and ask you a really hard question. *(Call one of the kids up front.)*

Now, you have two choices. I'm giving one of these away. You can either have the bag of cat litter or the three $1 bills. Which would you like to take home?

*(If the volunteer chooses the three $1 bills, open the bag of cat litter and pull the $20 bill out.)* Look what you missed! You see kids, this bag of cat litter looks like it doesn't have any value. I mean, you sure wouldn't want one of these for a Christmas present, right? But, inside this stinky bag of cat litter was a $20 bill.

*(If the volunteer chooses the bag of cat litter, say)* You made a good decision. Do you know why? *(Pull out the $20 bill.)* You didn't judge by appearances. Inside this "worthless" bag of cat litter is a $20 bill.

Kids, so often we judge people by the way they look. We think, "He isn't cool. Look at his shoes and the way he wears his pants. He's a real nerd." We need to learn to see people the way Jesus sees people. Jesus sees value in every person. There was something valuable in the bag of cat litter. Let's look for the value in each other and not judge each other by what we see on the outside.

Love

## Sky, Planets, Ocean and Time

**The Point:** God's love for us is immeasurable.

**Props:** Picture of the sky, ocean, planets or galaxy, clock, shoe box (or gift box), plastic storage bag and glass jar.

### PROCEDURE

Have you ever brought a part of the sky to school with you? How about a planet? Did you ever give a planet to somebody for a birthday present? Probably not. Have you ever told someone, "I would like to give you a piece of time?"

Each of these *(point to pictures and clock)*—the sky, the planets, the ocean and time—is immeasurable. You can't put the sky in a box. *(Hold up box.)* You can't put the ocean in a jar and bring it to school to tell your friends, "Here is the ocean." They would say, "You're crazy." And you can't store time in this storage bag *(put clock in bag)* and say, "I'll use this later when I don't have that much time."

The common thread between the sky, the ocean, the planets, galaxies and time is that they are all immeasurable. Have you ever taken a yardstick and tried to measure the sky or the ocean? No, because the sky and ocean are beyond measure—infinite.

Each of these *(point to pictures)* gives us a picture of God's love. The Bible says that God's love is infinite, limitless and unending. We can't even conceive of how big or how tall God's love is, because we can't measure it. Let's thank God for showing us His love through the sky, ocean, planets and time.

57

Love

## PROCEDURE

**G**od is just like this adhesive paper. *(Apply the adhesive paper to the posterboard.)* He will stick to you no matter what you do. *(Ask one of the kids to come up and try to tear it from the posterboard.)* You may do something and think, "Well, God has let me loose." Or, "I've offended God so much that He doesn't want to deal with me." This is how much God loves you. You can do all you want to try to let yourself loose from God, but He will continually stick to you.

You may think God has abandoned you, or He isn't around because you did a certain thing. Nothing you do can separate you from His love. The question is, will you receive His love? There's a Bible verse that describes His love "Yes, I am sure that nothing can separate us from the love God has for us. Not death, not life, not angels, not ruling spirits, nothing now, nothing in the future, no powers, nothing above us, nothing below us, or anything else in the whole world will ever be able to separate us from the love of God that is in Christ Jesus our Lord" (Rom. 8:38-39). And because He loves us, we need to share this love with others.

## Stick With Me

**The Point:** Nothing can separate us from the love of God.

**Props:** Wide adhesive paper (or tape) with "God" written on it and posterboard with "You" written on it.

## Jesus and Me

### PROCEDURE

**The Point:** Jesus sticks closer to us than any other friend.

**Props:** Two big pieces of cardboard with "Jesus" written on one and "Me" written on the other and fast-drying glue.

**Y**ou have friends in your neighborhood and friends at church who believe in you. But do you know who is your best friend who will stand with you even when others won't? Jesus. He is your best friend. *(Apply glue to the plain side of the cardboard pieces. Attach them together so that when you turn it one way it says "Jesus" and when you turn it the other way it says "Me.")*

Jesus will stick to you when others aren't around. *(Show both sides.)* He knows your heart. He knows your weaknesses. He knows every thought before you even think it. He has counted the hairs on your head, and He cares for you more than your parents could ever care for you.

So, kids, get to know this friend. He wants you to get to know Him. He wants you to know Him as a friend.

Love

## Incomplete Person

**The Point:** We are all members of one body.

**Props:** Posterboard, marker, scissors and bulletin board.

### PREPARATION

Make a large drawing of a face with two eyes, a nose, mouth. Cut it into different pieces to fit together like a puzzle or have the eyes, nose and mouth removable on a "blank face."

### PROCEDURE

Boys and girls, here is a face. *(Put an eye and nose on bulletin board.)* Isn't she pretty? No? Why? What's wrong with this picture? Is there anything missing? OK, let's add another eye. How's that? *(Point to picture.)* She sure is pretty, isn't she? What? Is this picture missing something again? OK, let's add the mouth. All right. Much better. How's that?

What happens if the mouth says to the nose, "Get lost, I don't need you!" *(Take nose off picture.)* Sure looks funny, doesn't it? Plus she couldn't smell. *(Put nose back on picture.)* Now, what if the eye says to the mouth, "I can make it on my own, I don't need you!" *(Take mouth off board.)* Boy, this sure looks funny again, doesn't it? Now this girl couldn't talk. She can see, but she can't talk. Let's put the mouth back on 'cause we know girls like to talk.

You know what? This is what the body of Christ is like. First Corinthians chapter 12 says we are the body of Christ. It says, "The eye cannot say to the hand—I don't need you!—and the head cannot say to the feet—I don't need you." We need each other to be complete. Each of us plays an important part, but we can't fulfill our roles unless other people are in their proper places. We are all different, with different roles, but we need each other. The eye needs the mouth to say what it sees. The nose needs the eyes to see what it is smelling. Let's accept each other by including one another.

## The Two Flowers

**The Point:** Treat others as you want to be treated.

**Props:** Two potted flowers, pin and scissors.

### PREPARATION

**H**ave one potted flower in front of the room on a table.

### PROCEDURE

Boy, isn't this flower beautiful? I love this flower. In fact, it's so pretty, I think I'll cut it off and wear it as a corsage. (Pin it on your shirt.) What do you think? Beautiful isn't it? But you know, this flower isn't going to last very long is it? Can anybody tell me what's going to happen to this flower? (Ask a few kids.) It's going to wilt and lose its petals eventually. Why? Because I cut it off. I wanted to use it just for myself. If I want more flowers, what should I do? (Have helper bring the other potted flower to the front.)

I need to take care of it. See this flower? It needs to be watered and fertilized if I want more pretty flowers. You know, that's how it is with people. If we want good friends, then we need to treat people the way we want to be treated. This flower is going to die because I used it. It made me look good temporarily, but in the long run, I've lost it. That's the way it is with people. You may benefit in the short term, but in the long run, you may have lost that friendship. When you use people, you lose.

## Gentle to All

**The Point:** We should be gentle toward others, just as Jesus is.

**Props:** Ragged clothes, wheelchair and cane. Note: Three actors are needed. One in wheelchair, one (elderly) walks with cane and one child in rags.

### PROCEDURE

Is there anyone in your school, your neighborhood or your family who has a serious physical problem? (*Push the person in the wheelchair to the front of the room.*) Maybe this person is in a wheelchair or on crutches. Maybe he is confined to bed, or perhaps he has cancer or a heart problem.

When someone has a physical problem, how is he treated by some people? He might be ignored, laughed at or looked down upon.

How would Jesus treat this person? What things could we do to treat this person with gentleness? (*Let the kids suggest answers to these two questions.*)

(*Now the person with the cane hobbles in.*) In our country, elderly people are often seen as less important than younger people. In many places, the elderly are treated with disrespect.

How would Jesus treat an elderly person? What things can we do to treat elderly people with gentleness? (*Again let the kids offer suggestions.*)

(*Have the poorly dressed child enter.*) If someone were to come to your school dressed like this, what would happen? (*Pause.*) If someone were to come to our church dressed like this, how would we treat him? (*Pause.*)

How would Jesus treat a child dressed in rags? What things can we do to be gentle to people who have less than we have? (*Kids suggest answers.*)

I know how Jesus would treat each of these people. He would be gentle with them. Will you follow Jesus' example?

## Healing

**The Point:** Jesus has provided for our healing.

**Props:** Coat, adhesive bandage strips (different sizes) and bandages.

### PROCEDURE

At times our bodies become weak and sick. Sometimes we do things that aren't smart, like playing outside without a coat on when it's cold. (*Your assistant enters wearing a coat.*) As a result, we sometimes become sick. (*Remove coat revealing numerous bandages on arms, elbows, etc.*)

Other times, you may fall down while skateboarding or running and get a terrible scrape. You need to bandage it up and take care of it. (*Point to bandages.*)

Other times, Satan will come against us, trying to make us ill. You see, in John 10:10 Jesus tells us that Satan comes "to steal and kill and destroy..." He enjoys seeing kids hurt. He even wants to destroy people.

(*Remove bandages during remainder of narrative.*) But that same Scripture continues on as Jesus says, "I came to give life—life in all its fullness." That means that even though Satan wants to destroy our lives, Jesus wants us to have the best life possible.

When Jesus took those stripes on His back, He provided for healing of our sicknesses. (*Remove bandage.*) If you have the flu, Jesus has already provided for that. (*Remove bandage.*) If you get pneumonia, Jesus has already provided for that too. (*Remove bandage.*) Whatever the problem, God has provided for your complete healing! (*Remove remainder of bandages.*) He wants you to have abundant life!

## Miraculous Powers

**The Point:** We will experience miracles through God's Holy Spirit.

**Props:** Different size batteries and flashlight (or battery-operated toy).

### PROCEDURE

Have you ever bought a battery for something and discovered it was the wrong size? A battery too large won't fit in the battery compartment. *(Show large battery.)* One too small won't have the power needed. *(Show small battery.)*

Have you ever wondered where the power comes from in a battery? Though it's hard to explain, we still know that the power is stored, waiting to be used.

In the same way, God has power that is stored and just waiting to be used. The Bible tells us that Jesus performed powerful miracles. He turned water into wine at a wedding in Cana. He stopped a raging storm. He raised Lazarus from the dead. Jesus had miraculous power! We don't understand it, but Jesus had power.

In the same way that this flashlight cannot produce light without the power of the right-sized battery inside, so we cannot do miraculous and great things for God without the power of His Holy Spirit inside of us. *(Put in the correct batteries and shine the light.)*

An exciting thing for each of us to remember is that the power of the Holy Spirit is for each of us. Jesus said in John 14:12, "He who believes in me will do the same things that I do. He will do even greater things than these..."

## PROCEDURE

**The Point:** Jesus does great things through us.

**Props:** Six glasses, blue and red food coloring and water pitchers (enough to fill each glass). Put blue and red food coloring in each glass ahead of time.

The first miracle Jesus performed was at a wedding party. Isn't it wonderful that a bride and groom loved Jesus and invited Him to be a part of their marriage? If all couples would invite Jesus into their marriages, there wouldn't be all the divorces, and families would be much happier.

At their wedding celebration, they ran out of refreshments. It was God's time for Jesus' first miracle. He often used something basic to start His miracles. This time He asked for six empty pots. They were big and held 20 to 30 gallons.

He told the servants to fill them with water. *(Pour water into the jars and stir so coloring shows.)* When they took the water from the jugs to the guests, the water had turned into fresh wine!

Jesus did this to reveal His glory. The disciples would then put their faith in Him. He is still using simple things and simple people to do great and mighty acts so others will put their faith in Him. Jesus might use you to be a part of His next miracle!

## PROCEDURE

### It's God Calling

**The Point:** God can speak to others through us.

**Prop:** Telephone.

Remember, prophecy's purpose is to build up, stir up and cheer up. Keep this in mind during this lesson.

*(Pick up the phone and have a conversation with someone.)* Hello. Uh-huh. Well. You don't say? You don't say? You don't say? *(Play with it a little.)* OK. Goodbye. *(Hang up.)*

One of the neat things about our living, loving God is that He wants to speak to us. He wants to help us to be strong for Him. He wants to keep us happy and "on fire" for Him. To tell us these things, He doesn't call us on the telephone. But He can speak to us and the entire congregation through one person.

When He uses one person to speak to the group, it is like receiving a telephone call and then telling others what the person said. When God calls through someone so that He can speak to the entire group of people, that's a prophecy.

He looks for someone to be his mouthpiece. God will give the words to say to build us up, to cheer us up or to get us moving again for Him. Being used by God in this way is one of the best things that could happen to us. One day in a service, God may call the church where you are worshiping, and He may call through you. So be ready!

## PROCEDURE

### New Marching Orders

**The Point:** Following Jesus means doing what He says.

**Props:** A large manila envelope with the words ORDERS - TOP SECRET written on it.

Every soldier gets orders. *(Hold up the envelope.)* He may not like it, but he is going to get orders and lots of them. To be a good soldier in any army, you must be able to take orders. Orders aren't just a bunch of do's and don'ts. They tell the soldier what to do and what not to do. But even more than that, they are for the good of the soldier and the entire army. If one soldier disobeys his orders, it could mess up the entire force.

When you ask Jesus to be your Commander in Chief, you are saying that you are willing to do whatever He asks you to do. If He says go, we must go. If He says wait, we must wait. He knows what is best for us. He knows more about us than we do.

Jesus gives us orders in many different ways. You probably will not receive orders from Jesus in an envelope like this. *(Show the envelope.)* His orders can come through the Bible. *(Hold up your Bible.)* It's a whole book of instructions for us.

When we pray, Jesus can speak to us in our hearts. Jesus can even use other people, like our pastor, Sunday School teachers or our parents to give us instruction. When He speaks to us, we must be willing to hear and obey what He tells us to do. We must do what our Commander in Chief says!

## PROCEDURE

**W**elcome to KIDS church. I'm excited today because I'm making my Ultimate Thirst Quencher. *(Begin the lesson by donning your "Galloping Gourmet" garb. Have fun with this one. The idea is to add to the directions on the package and mess up the recipe so badly that it is not drinkable. Do this by adding more or less of one ingredient than the recipe calls for. If the recipe calls for one cup of sugar, put in six cups, etc.)*

I'm really thirsty. *(Read the directions on the package.)* OH! My recipe is better than that! I'll mix up a batch of my very own special blend Ultimate Thirst Quencher. *(Start putting in ingredients. Exaggerate the addition of the ingredients and stir it.)*

Anyone want a drink? No? What do you mean, no? I know it's good. *(Pretend to take a taste, then pretend to spit it out.)* Yuk!

Hmm, I wonder what I did wrong. Maybe I shouldn't have added the Tabasco sauce *(or whatever you added)*. I guess I should have followed the recipe.

Every good soldier must follow instructions. As soldiers in God's army, we have to be able to follow instructions, too. God's instructions come to us in the Bible. We must be careful not to add to those instructions or change them, even if we think it would be better. We must follow the instructions very carefully, the way God gives them to us.

Obedience is very important for every soldier. We must obey what our Commander in Chief tells us to do. He has also put others in authority over us, such as our parents, teachers and pastors.

He knows what is best for us. Jesus won't lead us in the wrong direction.

**Obedience**

### PROCEDURE

**The Point:** Be a doer of the word.

**Props:** One dollar bill.

Over at the department store *(name a local store such as Sears, Penneys or Wal-mart)* the other day, I was picking up some important supplies. After I'd shopped for awhile and filled my basket, I headed for the check-out. The clerk rang up my items. The total was 16 dollars. I handed her a 20-dollar bill. She gave me my change, handed me a receipt and I left. When I got to my car, I looked at my change and noticed that I had been given five ones instead of four.

*(Hold up the dollar bill.)* I had an extra dollar! What should I do? I could go to McDonald's® and get some ice cream. I could go back into the store and get a candy bar. I had a free dollar! It was mine, and I didn't even have to work for it. The clerk messed up! It wasn't my fault. Praise God! Thank you, Jesus, for a free dollar!

Then I knew deep in my heart that it really wasn't mine. I hadn't earned it. It wasn't really given to me. It was a mistake. So I headed back into the store, not to buy a candy bar, but to return the dollar. The clerk was so surprised that I returned it. She said that she was responsible for the money. She would have had a dollar kept from her paycheck if I hadn't returned it.

I know I didn't have to return it. But I did because God wants me to be holy in the things I do. I did it to please Him. The sales clerk asked me why I didn't just keep the dollar like most people would. I told her that I'm a Christian and that God wants me to be holy in all my actions. . .even something as simple as returning a dollar that didn't belong to me. Now that sales clerk is going to know what a Christian is like because I showed her by my actions.

**Obedience**

## The Secret Scroll

**The Point:** Obeying God's rules leads to happiness.

**Props:** Two dowel rods, each about 18 inches long, and long strip of shelf paper (or newsprint).

### PREPARATION

Write an abbreviated version of the Ten Commandments on the paper. The version below has been modified for simplicity. At the end of the scroll, write "Your Friend, God." Prepare a scroll by taping one end of the paper to each dowel rod and then rolling it up.

1. Have no other gods before Me.
2. Do not make idols.
3. Do not misuse My name.
4. Remember the Sabbath day and keep it holy.
5. Honor your parents.
6. Do not murder.
7. Keep your body pure.
8. Do not steal.
9. Do not tell lies.
10. Don't be jealous of things others have.

Your friend, God

### PROCEDURE

If your group is small, you could say there is a "secret scroll" hidden somewhere in the classroom that has valuable, treasured data written on it. Let the children discover the scroll. Then read it to them as though this is top secret information!

Explain that these rules are God's secret for living a happy life. If we are God's friends, we will be obedient to these rules. We'll also help our own friends live by God's rules because we know they'll be happier if they do.

**Obedience**

## PROCEDURE

**The Point:** It's important to fill our minds with good things.

**Props:** Cassette player/recorder, blank cassette and volunteer.

Our minds have blank places in them that store what we hear. This cassette is blank. *(Put the cassette in and push "play" to show that it is blank.)* If we put this machine on "record," it will record what we say. *(Call up someone who can quote a verse of Scripture. Ask his name, a few other questions and then have him quote a verse. Stop the cassette.)* We teach people around us by what we say. Their minds are like a blank cassette, waiting to be filled with something. Will we put good things into their minds or bad things?

If this cassette were a mind, what would we have put in it? Let's play back the cassette now. *(Listen to the cassette.)* We put good things into it. What about our speech when we are at school or at play? Are the minds around us being filled with good things or bad? Let the Holy Spirit teach us and fill our minds with good things so we can teach others.

## PROCEDURE

### The Bad Dog

**The Point:** Rebellion leads to unhappiness.

**Props:** Dog collar, leash, dog toys, bone and stuffed dog.

Once upon a time there was a family with a mother, father and a small son. The mother and father decided their son would enjoy a dog. They bought him a soft, furry puppy. *(Hold up stuffed dog.)* Their son loved the puppy very much. They bought him a collar and a leash, some dog toys and some rawhide to chew on. *(Hold up each of the objects as you name them.)* The puppy loved to play.

As the puppy grew into a big dog, it became clear that he had a will of his own. When the son took him for a walk, the dog would tug and tug until he pulled the leash out of his master's hand. He'd run out into the street, right in front of cars. The dog chewed his toys and then started chewing the furniture. He hated baths and wouldn't stand still at all. At night he whined and cried, and no one could sleep. He had to be kept in the doghouse outside because he was so disobedient. The dog was so disobedient that the family couldn't enjoy him. The family decided to take their dog to obedience school. After a few weeks had passed, the dog had learned to obey his masters' commands. He got more walks because he had learned not to tug and run away. His baths were over quickly because he stopped struggling. He slept better and so did the family. He was allowed into the house again. Everyone was happier.

Sometimes boys and girls become like that puppy. It is very sad for the parents because they love their children and want to raise them in a happy home. Children will cry at bedtime, be messy, disobey rules and "break the leash." They rob their home of all joy when they are disobedient. The Bible says, "A rebellious child inherits the wind." That's not much of an inheritance, is it? You can't hold it in your hand, play with it or spend it. You can't even see it! Do you understand how disobedient kids are like the bad puppy in our story today? Do you want to be like that? Let's try to obey our parents in everything and see how much joy we can bring into our homes.

**Obedience**

## Chain of Command

**The Point:** Disobedience blocks blessings.

**Props:** A paper chain made from at least 15 strips of paper, each 3 inches long, scissors and tape.

### PREPARATION

**D**ecorate the first strip in the chain in some way to make it look important.

### PROCEDURE

In business, in school, in our homes and in the military, there is always a chain of command.
For example, our army is headed by the President of the United States. He is at the top as our Commander in Chief. Under him there are generals, then colonels, majors, captains, lieutenants, etc.

In the family of God there is also a chain of command. God is at the top. *(Hold paper chain up. Point to the decorated top link.)* The next is Jesus. *(Point to the second link.)* Moses was in the chain because God had established his authority. But people under Moses rebelled and were cut off from God's blessings. *(Choose a link about halfway down the chain and cut it. You will now have two chains.)*

*(Hold up both chains, visually demonstrating the separation from God in the bottom half of the chain.)* The Bible tells us that those who do not repent and get hooked up with God get in trouble. *(Cut off several more links from the bottom half of the chain.)* God has provided a way for us to get hooked up to Him again when we sin. If we repent and ask for His forgiveness, He is faithful to hook us up to the chain of command. *(Hold up a roll of transparent tape, indicating that it is like God's forgiveness. Hook the remaining links up to the "God chain" by taping them together.)*

We need to stay hooked up to God or we can be in big trouble. But to stay hooked up, we have to be obedient to God. If we want to stay hooked up to God and Jesus and their chain of command, we must stay obedient to Jesus. If we become disobedient *(cut a link from the bottom),* we cut ourselves off from God. If you disobey, come back to Jesus, repent and get hooked back up to His chain of command. *(Cut a link and then hook it back up with some tape.)*

## PROCEDURE

**The Point:** Bad thoughts pollute the mind.

**Props:** Large glass pitcher of water, mixing spoon, bottle of food coloring (red or blue) and bleach.

This glass pitcher is a mind with clean, pure thoughts. *(Pour in food coloring.)* But when we react to people, like your sister who ruined your book or your brother who called you a name, we begin to think unclean thoughts and bad ideas. We start thinking of ways of getting back at them instead of forgiving them. Once those thoughts and bad ideas are in our minds, they are polluted.

Now, would anyone like to come up and have a drink of this? Anybody out there thirsty for some food coloring and water? Nobody? Boys and girls, this is how our minds look when we lose control by reacting. Now, if you aren't in control, and God isn't in control, then who is? The devil. Let's take time to pray so we're alert and thinking clearly before we react to another person. How do we clean our minds when they're polluted? *(Add bleach to the colored water.)* By asking Jesus for forgiveness. Then Jesus can purify our minds and thoughts just as the bleach cleaned the water. Then we must fill our minds with the good things of God. Let's respond the way Jesus would.

## Buttons on a Shirt

**The Point:** Today's choices are tomorrow's destiny.

**Props:** Dress shirt.

### PROCEDURE

**L**ook at this nice shirt I'm going to wear today. *(Put the shirt on. Leave it unbuttoned.)*

Kids, *(begin buttoning shirt, but use the wrong order)* when we begin our lives, it's important that we start right. It's just like the shirt that I'm buttoning. All these buttons are out of order. How does this shirt look? Messy, doesn't it? Why does my shirt look so messy? *(Take a few answers.)*

Some of you are right. It's because I started with the wrong button. If you don't start with the right button at the bottom, then you end up with the wrong button on the top.

That's just like life. If we start out wrong, we may end up on the wrong road. The choices you and I make today will determine where we are tomorrow. That's why it is so important to follow Jesus now and get to know His voice. You are not too young to hear from the Lord and learn to recognize His voice. You are as responsible for your walk and salvation as your parents. If you stand before the Lord today and He asks you, "Why didn't you do this certain thing?" you can't answer, "Well, because I was too young." Kids, start out right by doing the right thing today.

## PROCEDURE

### Two Ways to Do Things

**The Point:** God's way is the best way.

**Props:** Two pieces of 2- by 3-foot posterboard and markers. Label one "My Way" and the other "God's Way."

**H**ave three workers share a brief personal account of a time in their lives when they tried to accomplish something without God. Have them stand under the "My Way" sign and talk about the way things got messed up when they insisted on having their way.

Make sure they emphasize that when they do things on their own, it's like setting themselves up in God's place in their lives. It's like making themselves a God. Then, one by one, have them stand underneath the "God's Way" sign and explain how much better things turned out when they began submitting to God.

## PROCEDURE

**Every** good soldier must be strong and healthy. Soldiers must work out with weights and practice with their weapons often. As soldiers in God's Army, we must be strong in the Lord. As soldiers, we must be skilled with all the weapons God has given us to use. We must be especially skilled with our secret weapon, the Holy Spirit. *(Begin lifting the barbells, making it look very difficult.)*

After you are filled with God's Secret Weapon, it's important to keep using this weapon. When we speak to God in our prayer language, the Bible tells us that we are building our spirit man up. It's like our spirit is lifting weights. Speaking in tongues makes our spirit strong. In the beginning, it may be hard to pray regularly, but the more you pray, the easier it becomes and the stronger you become. *(Lift the barbells, this time with ease.)*

The more we use this weapon, the stronger in the Lord we will be. God has given us this weapon to use. He has not given us this weapon to receive once and then get rid of it. Practice with your weapon every day, and be strong in the Lord.

## Spiritual Weightlifting

**The Point:** Praying to God will make us strong.

**Props:** Set of barbells. You can find inflatable barbells at many novelty or carnival supply stores.

**Prayer**

## PROCEDURE

**Building Up Your Faith**

**The Point:** Prayer makes our faith grow.

**Props:** Barbells. (Optional: Inflate two balloons and tie them to the ends of a stick.)

How many of you play soccer or baseball? *(Name a variety of sports.)* How many of you watch sports on tv? We can watch basketball, football, baseball, ice skating, wrestling and many other sports. Sometimes we can watch weight lifters compete. In the Olympics, weight lifters try to win the gold medal by lifting more weight than anyone else. These strong people can lift hundreds and hundreds of pounds. Often they lift more than two times their own weight.

Weight lifters are not born that strong. They develop that strength. Weight lifters work hours every day lifting barbells, kind of like these. *(Hold up barbells. Pretend to lift them over your head with great effort.)* As they work out with the weights, they get stronger and stronger.

Scripture tells us that we are to build ourselves up in our most holy faith. Then it tells us how to build up our faith by praying in the Holy Spirit. Our heroes of faith were not born spiritual giants, but as they prayed and trusted God they grew stronger and stronger in their faith. As we trust God and see His answers to our prayers, we will grow stronger, too. As we pray, God's Spirit inside our hearts will grow also.

It takes a lot of time to build strong enough muscles to win a weight lifting medal, and only a few win them. But we can be just like the heroes of faith by trusting God and building up our spirits. That's how we grow strong in faith.

## Fish or Stone

**The Point:** God always answers prayers.

**Props:** Fish sandwich and big stone.

### PROCEDURE

**K**ids, if you asked your mom or dad for a fish sandwich and they gave you a stone instead, what would you think? *(Let a few kids answer.)* Some of you would think, "Well my parents must not love me very much, because I asked for a fish sandwich and they gave me this stone." Now, you know your parents wouldn't do that to you, right?

Jesus says, "What would you do if your son asks for bread? Which of you would give him a stone? Or if your son asks for a fish, would you give him a snake? Even though you are bad, you know how to give good gifts to your children. So surely your heavenly Father will give good things to those who ask Him" (Matt. 7:9-11).

Your Father in heaven loves you so much that when you ask for a fish sandwich, He isn't going to give you a stone. *(Hold up the stone in one hand and the fish sandwich in the other.)* He may not respond immediately, and He might give you something that you need more than what you originally asked for. Kids, He has our best in mind, so let's trust Him and love Him, because He hears our prayers!

## PREPARATION

**W**rite on tag "Law" and place on smaller cup. Punch a hole in the bottom of the smaller cup. Draw a cross on the larger cup. Fill the water pitcher.

## PROCEDURE

**The Point:** We can do all things through Christ.

**Props:** Water pitcher, tag, marker, large bowl and two plastic cups. One cup should fit snugly in the other cup.

*(Pick up the cup that has a hole in it. Have the large bowl underneath.)* This cup reminds me of someone like you or me who tries to keep God's commandments through his own power.

*(Hold the cup over the large bowl. Pour water from the pitcher into the cup, letting it leak out the hole.)* This person knows God's commandments and tries to keep them, but he simply cannot do it. He may even have the Ten Commandments memorized, but there is a weakness in his life that causes his good intentions to just trickle away. His problem is that he is trying to serve God in his own strength.

*(Pick up the cup with the cross on it.)* Jesus wants to help this person. Jesus wants to live inside him so He can help him obey God's law.

*(Place the smaller cup inside the larger one.)* If that person or anyone else will believe and put his trust in Jesus, the Son of God will come to live inside him. Now watch what happens.

*(Pour water into the cup inside the cup.)* As this person relies on Christ, He is able to obey God's laws. Can he do this because of his own power? No! His new ability is coming from the perfect One living inside him—Jesus Christ!

Prayer

## PROCEDURE

**Fast Food**

**The Point:** Wait for the Lord's timing.

**Props:** Box of macaroni.

One of my favorite foods is macaroni. In fact, I think I'll have some right now! *(Try to eat some raw macaroni.)*

Yuck! That's awful! Uncooked macaroni just isn't the same as the finished product.

Of course, I should have remembered that. Once when I was a young kid, my mom was cooking dinner. I was so hungry that I slipped into the kitchen and got a piece of raw meat. I actually ate some of it! You can probably guess what happened, can't you? I got sick!

If I had just waited for her to cook that meat, it would have been nutritious and delicious. If I had waited until this macaroni had been cooked, it would have been yummy, too.

Some of the biggest mistakes that kids make in their lives happen when they decide, "I just can't wait!" When they go ahead and do something they're not ready for, they can ruin their lives.

Did you know that God has a special plan for your life? If you will wait for His timing, He will lead you into doing just the right things with just the right people at just the right time. So don't blow it! Wait for Him!

## PREPARATION

**M**ake a posterboard sign which reads "Handle With Prayer." Attach string to sign so it can hang around a child's neck.

## PROCEDURE

### Handle With Prayer

**The Point:** God's wants us to be gentle.

**Props:** Two pears (one ripe, one bruised and spoiled), posterboard and string.

We can learn about gentleness from pears. I like to eat pears because they are juicy and sweet. *(Take a bite from the ripe pear.)* But even though they feel firm, they actually are tender on the inside, so they bruise easily. That means that if a pear gets dropped on the floor, it will get a bad spot on it. That spot will turn brown, and the pear will start to go bad. *(Hold up the spoiled pear.)* When pears are packed for shipping, they aren't just thrown into a box. Why? Because the people who pack those pears know that they have to be gentle with them. They must not bruise them. That's why the containers that pears are shipped in are often stamped "Handle With Care." When the packers are gentle with them, the fruit stays sweet and juicy.

Now let's think about how we are like pears. I think people should wear signs that say "Handle With Prayer." *(Hang the sign around a volunteer's neck.)* We need people to pray for us. We need people to be gentle with us. We bruise just as easily as a pear.

Somebody will say a mean thing about you or laugh at the way you dress or the way you talk. That hurts you deep inside. It bruises you where no one else can see. Maybe your mom or dad curses at you, the kids in your neighborhood don't like you or your classmates pick on you. You need the people here at church to treat you with gentleness and to pray for you. Let's handle others with care and prayer.

## PROCEDURE

**The Point:** God is our helper.

**Props:** Telephone.

**W**hen I was old enough to leave home, my mom told me that if I ever needed anything, all I would have to do would be to call her on the phone. That was a comforting thing for me to hear. *(Make a call. Hold the receiver and mimic dialing the phone as you describe each need to make a call.)*

No matter what kind of trouble I was in, I could count on my mom to be there for me. I needed that assurance when I first left home. I didn't know how to take care of myself that well.

I knew that if I ever had a question, all I had to do was pick up the phone, call my folks and ask. I knew they would be there to help. One time I got into a little trouble. *(Make a call.)*

It wasn't easy to make the call. This wasn't a happy, "Hello, how are you?" type of phone call. I did make the call.

I called my parents, and they were there to save me. But I want to tell you about something even better than that. You see, God is just like a parent in that regard. He said that if you ask Him to help, He will be there to save you. But we have to call on Him. We have to ask Him. What would have happened if I didn't call on my parents to help me when I needed it?

*(Put telephone away and help children focus on your words.)*

If I hadn't made the call, I wouldn't have gotten the help, right? It was there for me. Think about it.

God is always there for us, but I believe that, even though God can save us and wants to save us, many people aren't saved because they don't ask. We have to make the call. Our answer is to call on Him. He promises never to leave us, and His promise invites us to call Him.

### PROCEDURE

### The Closest One

**The Point:** Don't hesitate to pray.

**Props:** Fire extinguisher.

**W**here is the best place to keep a fire extinguisher? *(Hold up the fire extinguisher.)* You will see a number of fire extinguishers around church, at your school and other public places. It's a safety item to have in our homes.

Where is the best place to have a fire extinguisher when a fire actually breaks out? There's only one correct answer—CLOSE!

There will be times in your life when you are the best answer to a problem or need because you are close. You might be the closest one when your mom or dad needs prayer. Don't wait to tell the pastor that your parents need prayer. You pray. You are the closest. Don't miss the chance to do something great for God....you pray!

You are valuable because you are the closest one to the problem. It's too easy to think that God can't use you and let that be an excuse for not doing anything. God can use you. He wants to use you. He thinks you are valuable.

Because God created you and you are valuable to Him, He places you close to others. You are His answer. You are valuable.

## Dirty Water

**The Point:** Jesus makes us pure.

**Props:** Clear glass of water, spoon and some dirt.

### PROCEDURE

Our lives are like this glass of water. When we give our lives to Jesus, He changes us and makes us pure like Him. As we go about our lives and stay holy and separate from sin, we continue to be useful to God. *(Take a sip of the water.)* It is very important that we stay clear of things that are displeasing to God.

Sometimes in our daily living we are tempted to do things that are not pleasing to God, and we sin. *(Toss a spoonful of dirt into the glass.)* Sometimes we are tempted to lie or steal or disobey our parents. *(With each sin you mention, drop a spoonful of dirt in the glass.)*

Sin can keep us from being useful to God. You wouldn't want to drink this glass of water now, would you? Of course not! Sin affects our spiritual appearance. Sin can keep us from being the best representatives for Jesus.

We must keep ourselves free from sin. We must remember that we are representing Jesus in everything we do and live holy lives that are pleasing to Him. Even though this glass of water looks clean on the outside, the water is not drinkable because there's dirt on the inside.

God wants you to be holy on the inside, too. Some people think that being holy means wearing old clothes, living alone in a cave or performing rituals that have nothing to do with what is in your heart or what you are. When you are holy on the inside, cleansed from sin, God will take care of the outside.

## PREPARATION

**P**unch holes in each tag and attach a piece of yarn so you can hang the price tag around a child's neck. Make a 5th tag larger or more colorful than the rest that reads: "Wholly Holy 100% Sold Out to God!" On the other tags, write:

| (Side A) | (Side B) |
|----------|----------|
| Trustworthy | Rummage |
| Faithful | 50% off |
| Valuable | Discounted |
| Treasure | Clearance |

## PROCEDURE

*(Choose four children to come forward and participate in this activity.)* We are prized by God. He sees us as trustworthy, faithful, valuable and treasure. *(Hang the tags around the children's necks.)*

When we allow sin in our lives, it makes us feel as if we are of very little value. If we are dishonest or disobey, we might feel as if we are rummage. *(Turn the trustworthy tag over.)* Some people are not faithful about church worship. This sin in their lives might make them feel they should be labeled "50% off." *(Turn the faithful tag over.)* Fifty percent dependable and fifty percent undependable. Other people have let sin stain their lives in so many ways that they don't know their true worth. *(Turn the valuable tag over.)* Some people think they should be wearing a "Discounted" tag because of the flaws and stains sin has left on their lives. Others think that they are so full of sin that God just wants to get rid of them. *(Turn the treasure tag over.)*

Boys and girls, those are all sin's lies. God loves us and cares for us. He wants us to get rid of the sins in our lives so we can see our own true worth. *(Turn all of the tags over again.)* We are all valuable to Him. But people can choose whether they want to be "sold out" 100% to God or be slaves to sin. Selling out to sin is no bargain! It only makes us feel bad about ourselves.

## Discount Items

**The Point:** Sin blinds us from knowing God's love.

**Props:** Four large paper or posterboard "price tags" about 18 by 24 inches.

## PROCEDURE

# Don't Cheat

**The Point:** Lying is a sin before God.

**Props:** Board game (such as Monopoly®) and some "funny money." (You can make a transparency of a gameboard and show it on the overhead.)

**H**ere's the set-up. You and your friend have been playing this game for awhile. *(Have a child come up to play against you in the board game.)* Your friend is winning. He excuses himself for a minute to go to the bathroom. *(Child leaves.)* While he is gone you look at the board. It's worse than you thought! You decide to even out the game a little bit. You take some money from the bank and move your piece closer to the winning spot. *(Move money to your side of the board.)*

What's happened? You've cheated! You are lying to your friend. You know what you've done is wrong.

Many people think that lying is only a sin if you get caught, but remember, God sees all of our actions. So every time we don't tell the truth, whether we get caught or not, God knows it. Lying is a sin and we must be trustworthy before God even when no one else is looking.

It's easy to lie. It would be easy to win that way. But we know that God is displeased with lying. We know the truth about lying. It is a sin. We must be trustworthy before God even when nobody is looking. People of God are holy in all things.

## Mouth Control

**The Point:** Lying hurts others and God.

**Props:** 12- to 15-inch balloon.

### PROCEDURE

Is lying a big deal? *(Have a helper begin blowing up the balloon as you talk. When you give a pre-arranged cue, she is to release the balloon.)* What if your mom tells you that you have to vacuum the living room before you can go outside and play? The living room doesn't look that dirty, so you stand there with the vacuum cleaner on. A few minutes later you turn it off and tell your mom you vacuumed the living room. She lets you go outside and play.

Now, what you have just said is a lie. You might not think it's that big of a deal, but one lie can lead to another. You have basically lost control of your mouth. If you're not in control, and God doesn't lie, then who is in control? The devil.

Once we tell a lie, it's hard to know where it will end. *(Cue volunteer to release the balloon.)* Once you tell one lie, it's hard to go back and straighten it out with the truth. But if you have told a lie, you need to go back and tell the truth, even if it is difficult. The best choice is to not lose control of your mouth by lying. You might think it isn't going to hurt anybody, but a lie hurts God.

## PROCEDURE

## Glamorous Ads

**The Point:** It's dangerous to flirt with sin.

**Props:** Advertisements for cigarettes, beer and wine, cigarette butt, beer can and wine bottle.

**K**ids, see these ads? *(Hold up the ads you've brought in.)* They make smoking cigarettes and drinking beer and wine look really fun and glamorous. You always see pretty ladies, handsome men and boats or race cars in these ads. But what these ads don't tell you is that cigarettes cause cancer and bring death to many people. These beer and wine ads don't show the millions of people who are hurt emotionally or physically by family members who are alcoholics, or the thousands of people who die every year because of drunk drivers.

Sin looks glamorous and seems like fun at the beginning, but then it progresses and controls you. Sin is a harsh master, as shown by the families that are hurt by alcoholism or the people who die from cancer. And sin can begin with just one cigarette *(hold up cigarette butt)*, or just one beer *(hold up beer can)* or one glass of wine *(hold up wine bottle)*. When people start smoking cigarettes, their goal isn't to get cancer. When people start drinking, their goal isn't to go out and kill somebody by driving drunk.

No, it begins because you think it's fun and cool to look older by smoking and drinking. You start with just a little bit...one cigarette, one beer, one glass of wine. Before you know it, you want another cigarette. You want another beer and another glass of wine.

Then it begins to get hold of you, and before you know it, you need it. You need the next cigarette and the next beer or glass of wine. That's when it gets dangerous. It begins as a fun thing, but then it gets control of you. Kids, don't give room to sin! Now I'm not just talking about cigarettes and alcohol. These are just examples to show you the evil effects of sin. But you need to read the Bible and ask God to show you areas of sin in your life you need to put away.

## Thread Around the Wrist

**The Point:** Repeated sin becomes a habit.

**Props:** Spool of thread and large pair of scissors labeled "Repentance."

## PROCEDURE

Kids, this piece of thread represents sin. *(Have a volunteer from the congregation come and wrap the piece of thread around your wrist and tie it.)* You can do it once, and it doesn't seem like it would be hard to stop. *(Break the piece of thread.)* See, it's real easy. But what would happen if you continually did it, over and over again? *(Ask a volunteer from the congregation to come up and wrap the thread around your wrist 15 to 20 times.)*

You may think, I can get away with it just this one time. But if you do it over and over again *(have volunteer tie the thread around your wrist)*, and you try to break it *(ask the volunteer to try to break the thread)*, you can't break it. You can try all kinds of things to try to stop the sin. But because you have done it over and over again, it becomes a habit that you can't break.

What can set you free? *(Ask volunteer to take scissors and cut off thread.)* Repentance. True repentance is asking God to forgive you and turning away from the sin. The Bible says that the truth will set you free. The truth convicts you of your sin, and repentance breaks its power. Kids, don't let sin deceive you into thinking that you can do it once and get away with it. If you are already ensnared, then repent, ask God to forgive you and don't do it again!

## PREPARATION

**From Anger to Murder**

**The Point:** Anger leads to murder. *(Read Matthew 5:21-22.)*

**Props:** Four boxes of graduated sizes which can be placed inside each other.

Label the smallest box "Anger"; the next to smallest, "Hate"; the next-to-largest, "Fights"; and the largest, "Murder."

## PROCEDURE

*(Hold the box labeled "Anger" in your hand. The other three boxes should be kept out of sight until each one is needed.)*

It's very easy to get angry with someone. We all do it. Have you ever gotten angry at your parents? A brother or sister? A friend? A teacher? Someone who doesn't like you? When we have feelings of "Anger," we must be very careful, for anger can easily lead to sin. We must not keep anger in our hearts for long. We must get rid of it, or it will lead to something worse.

*(Bring out the box labeled "Hate.")* If we do not deal with our anger quickly, we give the devil an opportunity to turn our anger into hatred. *(Place the "Anger" box inside the "Hate" box.)* Hatred is a terrible sin. You might begin to hate someone because of something he said or did, because of the color of his skin, because of where he lives or even because of the school he attends.

*(Bring out the box labeled "Fights.")* If we hate someone, we will eventually try to hurt that person. Hatred leads to fighting. *(Place the "Hate" box inside the "Fights" box.)* We will fight that person with our tongue by saying cruel things about him...then we might fight that person with our fists...and we might even use a weapon to fight him!

*(Bring out the box labeled "Murder." Place the "Fights" box inside it.)* Some people begin to hate someone so much that they even kill that person. You might think, I could never commit murder! But we do not know for sure what we might do if we let Satan control our lives.

The best way to be sure you never commit such a terrible sin is to not get involved in fights. *(Remove the "Fights" box from the "Murder" box.)* The best way to avoid getting in fights is to refuse to hate anyone. *(Remove the "Hate" box.)* And the best way to keep from hating is to learn to get rid of anger when it rises up. *(Remove the "Anger" box.)*

## PREPARATION

**W**rite "Lie" on each piece of paper and attach tape to the back.

## PROCEDURE

### I Lie + I Lie = Liar

**The Point:** Little lies can grow.

**Props:** Fifteen pieces of paper and double-sided tape.

I need a volunteer. *(Bring up a child and ask her name. As you tell the story, add pieces of paper to her body until much of her body is covered with "lies.")*

Jenny looks like a pretty nice kid. She doesn't look like a liar to me. Well, let's pretend that she gets herself in a bind and she decides to tell a lie. Just one. *(Put one piece of paper on child's body.)*

Remember when you tell one lie, you usually tell another lie to cover that one up. *(Take another piece of paper and place over the first one.)* So now you've got two lies! One lie leads to another, which leads to still another lie. *(Start sticking the pieces of paper all over the child's body so he is completely covered.)*

Now look at what you have become...a liar! Why? Because you are covered in lies. It always starts out small, but, boy, how fast it can grow.

Do you remember when I told you that one lie can become a habit, which in turn can become a lifestyle of lying? Did you know that the opposite of a lie is truth? You will never do better than to tell the truth. Truth will never let you down. The devil will let you down, and lying is letting the devil take hold of your life. God says "Do not lie." All you have to do is ask God to forgive you when you lie and He will. God loves us and He wants us to do our very best for Him.

## A Nickel and Dime Death

**The Point:** Small sins can have big consequences.

**Props:** Nickel, dime and posterboard.

### PREPARATION

**W**rite the words "tiny sin" in small letters next to the word "DEATH" written in large letters on the posterboard.

### PROCEDURE

I am going to show you how a little sin can turn into death. *(Carry the poster around the room as you say this.)*

It may seem impossible for one little wrong, or sin, to ever turn into something big—especially death. The truth is that most big events have small beginnings. *(Hold up the nickel and dime.)* Here's the evidence. This nickel and dime represent a little beginning that ended in death—15 cents that ended a life.

Ace was a young boy who was always in a hurry to get whatever he wanted. After all, "You've got to make your own way in this world," Ace would say. "Take what you want, just don't get caught." The worst thing about what Ace was saying was that it worked for him. He was getting his way, or so it seemed.

The nickel and dime represent what Ace took from his mother's purse. Little needs grow into big needs. Ace just started taking whatever he needed whenever he needed it. This led to the day Ace and some of his friends felt like a little joy ride. Of course, they didn't have a car. No problem for Ace; he knew the answer—just don't get caught.

This story would have a happier ending if Ace and his friends had just been arrested for stealing, but that's not how it went. The trip for Ace and his friends ended in a car accident. Nobody walked away from the accident. The ride ended in death.

It seems impossible, but this nickel and dime taken in sin can end in death. Little sins can lead to death. We need to turn from sin and not allow ourselves to believe that we can get away with it.

## PREPARATION

**F**ill jar to the brim with colored water. Place jar on the baking pan to catch the overflow of water.

## PROCEDURE

### Fill 'Er Up!

**The Point:** Feed your faith.

**Props:** Clear glass jar, colored water, yellow aquarium gravel (or sand) and baking pan.

You want to cut the roots of sin. How do you do it? Look at this glass. The colored water represents our habit of doing things that aren't right. So what we have here is a life filled with bad habits.

What's the best way to get rid of that colored water? Unfortunately, we can't just turn ourselves upside down and watch all the sin come out of our ears. No, there's a better way to do it. *(Start to add gravel to the glass.)*

What we're going to do is add gravel and start to make some real changes. Let's imagine this yellow gravel represents good things. Sounds better already! Each and every tiny piece of gravel here represents one good thing you can add to your life. It sure is an improvement over all the colored sin. Does adding one good thing get rid of all those habits? No, but it's a start in the right direction.

Let's add some more gravel. As the gravel goes into the glass, guess what happens to the water? The water comes out. It's being pushed out. The more gravel we add, the more water comes out. If we fill the glass with gravel, there won't be any room left for water.

If we fill our lives with good things like prayer, Bible study, church and godly friends, there won't be any room left for sin habits. Feed the good side, and it will grow. Starve the bad side, and it will die.

## Angelic Bodyguards

**The Point:** God's angels protect us.

**Props:** Roll of brown shipping paper (or paper large enough to trace outline of child), glue, scissors and posterboard (or cardboard box).

## PREPARATION

**B**efore class, trace child's outline, glue it to the posterboard and cut it out.

## PROCEDURE

God has always had His own way of protecting His people. The angels are God's secret police. We will call them "God's bodyguards." *(Bring a child to the front and place him in front of the silhouette.)*

In Exodus 14:19, God's bodyguards traveled in back of His people to protect them, and then they went in front of His people. In Psalm 91:11, God commands His bodyguards to guard you in all your ways. In Daniel 6:22, God's bodyguard shut the lions' mouths to protect Daniel in the lions' den. *(In each instance bring a child forward to stand in front of the silhouette.)* The angels stand before and behind us to protect us from the attacks of the enemy. They are like a shield of protection.

## What Do We Wear?

**The Point:** Put on the armor of God.

**Props:** Lots of clothes: shirts, pants, gloves, hats, sweaters, ear muffs, scarves, etc.

## PROCEDURE

I'm getting dressed today to prepare myself for the problems I may have to face. I need lots of protection and warmth. *(Put on garments as you talk, one on top of another, gloves, pants, shirts, etc.)* Yes, nothing can touch me because I am so well padded and insulated! No one can see or touch my body. What a bunch of protection and armor I have! No one can hurt me. Nothing can get to me. A bullet couldn't pierce its way through all of this. A knife couldn't cut through all these layers. If I fall down, I won't get bruised or skinned.

Wait a minute! The Bible says to put on the armor of God!. This isn't God's armor. This is my own armor. Besides, I am not going to fight people. I am supposed to wear God's armor because my enemy is the devil!

I have to protect my insides—my spirit, my heart and my mind against the temptations to sin and the suggestions and lies from the devil. Sadness can get through all these clothes, can't it? Rebellion can get through, too. These clothes can't protect me from getting mad or angry.

*(Have a boy look up 2 Corinthians 10:4 and read it for the kids. Have a girl look up Romans 13:12 and read it.)* His Word, the Bible, will dress our hearts and our thoughts with power to win this battle.

## A Blinding Reflection

**The Point:** Righteous living makes us shine.

**Props:** A clear, shiny mirror, some dirt and window cleaner.

### PROCEDURE

Our Breastplate of Righteousness is bright and shiny like this mirror. *(Hold up the mirror.)* When the light hits the mirror and reflects off it, the light can almost be blinding to our eyes. *(Try to show a bright light reflecting in the mirror. You may need to set up a special light like a small spotlight.)* When we serve Jesus with all of our hearts and do not sin, we stay in righteousness and we keep our breastplates clean and shiny. When our breastplates are clean, our enemy doesn't want to get around us. The devil flees from righteousness. He hates that kind of bright light.

But if we sin, we dull our breastplate. *(Wipe some dirt on the mirror to dull it.)* Sin keeps us from being as strong and protected as we need to be. *(Show the dirty mirror.)* When we put on our armor, it is important for us to make sure our breastplates are clean. We can keep them clean, bright and shiny by trusting Jesus to forgive us of our sins (1 John 1:9). And if our breastplates get dirty, we need to ask for His forgiveness as soon as we realize that we have done something that Jesus doesn't like. He will help us clean our breastplates. *(Spray cleanser on the mirror and begin to wipe it clean.)*

Knowing that we can clean our breastplates when we need to does not give us permission to mark them up whenever we want to. Boys and girls, we need to hate the sin that the devil tempts us with just as much as Jesus hates it. *(Hold up the clean mirror.)* Kids, please keep your Breastplates of Righteousness clean and shiny.

## PROCEDURE

**C**an you imagine if your teacher told you tomorrow morning that Tuesday morning you were going to have a test covering this book and anyone who didn't pass it would flunk your grade? *(Open the book and read a sentence or two, something really technical. Make it sound really confusing.)*

You'd be upset, huh? You would stay up all night trying to figure out how to pass the test. You would sweat and fret, and fret and sweat, and still not be able to pass. It's just too hard.

Getting to heaven is like that test. We try and try on our own but can't do it. We can be really uneasy and confused inside. There is no peace inside; we can't rest.

When Jesus becomes our Commander in Chief, He helps to make those uneasy and confused feelings go away. We feel at peace with God.

Many things can happen that can bring on that uneasy feeling again. When we obey the devil and sin against God, we can lose our peace. When we do sin, we can ask Jesus to forgive us and He will restore our peace. Even without sinning, Satan can lie to us and confuse us. That's why we need to be protected with God's peace.

When Jesus rose from the dead, He destroyed the devil's power over us. Jesus' peace helps us to know that the devil's tales are a bunch of hot air.

## I'm Soooo Confused!

**The Point:** Jesus gives us peace.

**Props:** A thick college textbook on a difficult subject, like calculus or advanced biochemistry (or make a fake book cover).

**Warfare**

## Footprints

**The Point:** We should follow in Jesus' footsteps.

**Props:** Cut out ten poster-board footprints.

### PROCEDURE

People dislike their feet. If you asked most people what part of the body they think is most unattractive, they would say, "My feet!" A lot of people have aching feet. *(Each time you are directed to hold up a footprint, first hold it up for everyone to see, then place it on the floor to make a path. Hold up the first footprint now.)* No wonder, for one-fourth of all the bones in your body are in your feet. *(Hold up a footprint.)* There are 54 bones, 19 muscles and 100 ligaments and tendons. *(Hold up a footprint.)* The average American walks *(hold up a footprint)* 70,000 miles in a lifetime! *(Hold up a footprint.)* "When a man's steps follow the Lord, God is pleased with his ways." (Ps. 37:23). *(Hold up a footprint.)* God is so interested in your feet He has counted your footsteps (Job 31:4). *(Hold up a footprint.)* "God sees my ways, and he counts every step I take."

The walk of a soldier is very important because he could step on mines *(hold up a footprint)* the enemy has placed in the war zone. We have to walk in the light and not in sin's darkness (1 John 1:7); and *(hold up a footprint)* not walk in the advice of the ungodly (Ps. 1). Make sure your friends are people who love the Lord!.

People may think their feet are ugly, but God doesn't think so. Especially the Christian soldier's feet. Do you know what God says about feet? *(Hold up a footprint)* "How beautiful on the mountain are the feet of them that bring good news..."

Take a look at your feet, kids. Let's decide to use our feet to walk in the way God wants us to. *(Call attention to the path of footprints you have created on the floor.)* Let's stay on His paths.

## PROCEDURE

### Turtle Protection

**The Point:** Faith is our shield against the enemy.

**Props:** Turtle (or picture or stuffed animal).

**L**ook at the top of this turtle. *(Show the turtle.)* Have you ever touched the top of a turtle? I am sure you have. It is hard, isn't it? The turtle's shell is its protection. It is strong enough to keep the turtle safe in the woods from falling branches or even other animals. Have you ever snuck up on a turtle? What happens when the turtle sees you for the first time? The turtle hides himself inside his shell. He pulls his head, legs and tail inside. He does not know for sure what you may do. He knows what his shell will do; it will protect him. He knows that he will be safe from his enemy. He is completely protected.

When we dress ourselves in the armor of God, we put on our Shield of Faith. God's shield is so big that it completely covers us. We can hide behind the shield. We can be protected from our enemy's bullets with the shield. This shield is strong, too. It is tough enough that it can put out fire.

Satan will shoot fiery arrows of fear or discouragement at you. We need to know that these fiery feelings are not coming from God. When we hide behind our shield, we trust God to take care of us. His shield puts out all the fire of the enemy.

Kids, we can hide completely behind our shield and know God will help us conquer the enemy's lies of fire.

## PREPARATION

**M**ake a large cardboard heart with a handle taped to the back of it to resemble a heart shield. Label darts: No answer to prayers, Curses, Troubles, Loneliness, Sickness.

## PROCEDURE

## Shield of Faith

**The Point:** We must always be on guard.

**Props:** Cardboard, tape and darts.

*(Ask for five volunteers to help.)* In the fight of faith, God's soldiers are sometimes attacked by fiery darts from the enemy. These fiery darts can be bad thoughts that come to your mind, or they can be problems that other people bring. You can stop those darts with the Shield of Faith. When troubles and fiery darts come, put up your Shield, which is putting your faith and belief in God, right out in front of you.

*(Give one of the kids the dart labeled "No answer to prayers." Have them hold it, aiming—but not throwing—right at the shield.)* That was the dart from the enemy that says my prayers won't get answered. But my Shield of Faith, my belief in God, has stopped it. *(Give another boy or girl the dart labeled "Curses." Again, have them hold it, aiming, but not throwing, right at the shield.)* Sometimes the devil puts bad words in your mind, or people may curse in front of you. Put up your Shield of Faith. Believe in blessing words and bless out loud every time you hear a curse. *(Have another boy or girl bring the "Troubles" dart to the shield, again holding and aiming, but not throwing the dart at the shield.)* Troubles can be stopped and turned into treasured times. *(Repeat as above with "Loneliness" dart.)* Loneliness can become a friendship with the Lord and others. *(Repeat as above with "Sickness" dart.)* The Sickness dart can be stopped and turned into wellness.

Nobody puts his shield in a closet or under the bed. A soldier has his shield with him at all times. Always be on guard because your Shield of Faith will be your protection. Kids, take up the Shield of Faith against the devil's darts.

## PROCEDURE

**The Point:** The word of God is a weapon against the devil.

**Props:** Real (or toy) sword and Bible.

There comes a time in every soldier's life when he has to quit taking it from the enemy and *attack*!

The enemy will be firing on you, and you may be well protected. The enemy may not even be coming close to hurting you because of your protection. But you still have to fight.

Satan has been shooting his fiery arrows at you. Your shield has protected you. He has hit your head, and your helmet has kept you safe. Your breastplate has protected your heart. But don't just take it from him, fight!

God has given us a weapon. It's the best weapon there is to use against our enemy. It's the Sword of the Spirit. It does damage, not just by swinging it from side to side, but by stabbing it in.

God's sword is the Bible, with the truth inside its pages. Now you can't hit Satan over the head with this book. *(Hold up Bible.)* That won't hurt him. What will hurt him is when you study this book and memorize its words. Then when you get under attack by the enemy, you can come out fighting. Give him some of God's Word that you have memorized. He hates it. God's Word will defeat the enemy every time.

Kids, hold your swords *(Bibles)* up in the air. This sword is one of the pieces of armor we must put on daily. Don't forget this final piece of armor.

## PREPARATION

**T**he idea you want to convey is that you are good at what you do because you have practiced and done it over and over and over. If you have trouble coming up with an idea, bring in a sneaker and demonstrate tying your shoe.

## "Look, Mom, I can do it!"

**The Point:** We should memorize God's Word.

**Props:** Bring something you do well, such as yo-yos, juggling, knitting or art.

## PROCEDURE

Doing this used to be difficult for me. *(Demonstrate your skill.)* I didn't think I'd ever get the hang of it. I had to practice many, many hours to be able to do this. I still have to practice. If I don't practice, I won't be as good as I am now. I will lose some of my ability. *(Stop demonstrating your skill.)*

As a little boy, Jesus went to Sunday School and church just like you do today. His church was a little different, but He still learned about the Bible and God. He studied the Bible a lot. He learned its truth, and He memorized it.

Satan tried to defeat Jesus when He lived on the earth. Jesus was attacked by the devil many times. Every time Jesus was attacked, Jesus used His weapon, His sword, to fight back against Satan. He had practiced with that sword many times and was good at using it. Every time the enemy tried to get Jesus to do something, Jesus knew it was wrong. He knew it was wrong to do because He had studied and memorized God's Word. So when attacked, He could tell Satan, "I can't do that because God's Word says. . ."

Jesus knew that God's Word was the only offense He had against the enemy. It is our offense, too. God's Word is all we need when we are attacked. We will be good at fighting the devil by practicing and using our weapon, the Sword of the Spirit.

## PREPARATION

On posterboard, draw a large profile of a head with scribbling representing the brain. Cut out a door with a doorknob and attach it to the center of the brain so the door can open and close.

## PROCEDURE

**A Head Problem**

**The Point:** Guard your thoughts.

**Props:** Posterboard and marker.

The helmet protects the head. *(Show the head drawn on posterboard.)* Our entire victory comes from what is brought from the head: thoughts and words. Orders are taken from listening ears and seeing eyes. Revelation 12:11 states that Christians won the battle by their words. If your head goes unprotected, the battle against evil is lost forever.

Hope is in the head. It is not in the heart. It is because hope enters the brain that faith can come into the heart. People who give up and quit always lose hope first. Let's open the door to hope. *(Open the door cut into the poster-board head.)*

Hope will not stay long if rude visitors are allowed to come in and make themselves at home in the mind. That is why Paul said in Philippians 4:8 to only let certain visitors in the mind, "things that are good and worthy of praise...that are true and honorable and right and pure and beautiful and respected." Set a burglar alarm and wear a Helmet of Salvation to keep bad visitors from coming in.

Salvation is a "head protection experience!" Don't let bad thoughts in the door. *(Close the door.)* If they are allowed to come in and hang out for a while, they will leave through the mouth. Thoughts come in, turn into words and come out the mouth. That's why we wear the Helmet of Salvation. *(Open the door.)* Having Jesus in the head means good thoughts and good words are at home in the mind.